PELIC

ROME BEYOND TH

SIR MORT

ROME
BEYOND THE IMPERIAL
FRONTIERS

BY

SIR MORTIMER WHEELER

PENGUIN BOOKS

Penguin Books Ltd, Harmondsworth, Middlesex
U.S.A.: Penguin Books Inc., 3300 Clipper Mill Road, Baltimore 11, Md
CANADA: Penguin Books (Canada) Ltd, 47 Green Street,
Saint Lambert, Montreal, P.Q.
AUSTRALIA: Penguin Books Pty Ltd, 762 Whitehorse Road,
Mitcham, Victoria
SOUTH AFRICA: Penguin Books (S.A.) Pty Ltd, Gibraltar House
Regent Road, Sea Point, Cape Town

—

First published 1954
Published in Pelican Books 1955

Made and printed in Great Britain
by Wyman & Sons Ltd
London, Reading, and Fakenham
Collogravure plates by
Harrison & Sons

CONTENTS

PART THREE: ASIA

ILLUSTRATIONS

TEXT FIGURES

PLATES

PREFACE

THIS little book first took shape on a hot May morning in 1945, when an Indian student of mine emerged excitedly from a deep trench beside the Bay of Bengal waving a large slice of a red dish in his hand. Removal of the slimy sea-mud revealed the dish as a signed work of a potter whose kilns flourished nearly 2,000 years ago and 5,000 miles away, on the outskirts of Arezzo in Tuscany. Were drama admissible to the archaeological scene, I should have been tempted to describe the moment as dramatic. In that moment the pages of the historians and the geographers leapt to life; the long, acquisitive arm of imperial Rome became an actuality.

Elsewhere in the East, the discovery of Roman things, or their more local simulacra, has outpaced adequate record in recent years. The reason lies partly in the accident that few orientalists have been trained in the classical school, and that the significant Western material therefore, when found, is not always recognized. The present book does not profess to fulfil this need in any comprehensive sense. It is not an archaeological gazetteer, such as is now badly wanted; but it may at least serve summarily to indicate the scope of the problem and to invite further attention to those matters.

For the West, the field has been admirably surveyed, for some time to come, by Dr H. J. Eggers in his monumental work on Roman imports into Free Germany, published while this book was in preparation. With Dr Eggers's generous permission, I have drawn freely upon his material, particularly for my maps. To many others I am likewise greatly indebted for illustrations: especially to Dr H. C. Broholm of Copenhagen, to Dr G. Caputo, lately head of the Archaeological service in Libya, to Monsieur M. Reygasse of the Bardo, Algiers, to Mrs Olwen Brogan and the Society for the Promotion of Roman Studies, to Mr J. B. Ward Perkins, Director of the British School at Rome, to the Archaeological Department of the Government of India, to the late Director of the Baroda Museum and Picture Gallery, and to the German Archaeological Institute.

MORTIMER WHEELER

Institute of Archaeology
  University of London, 1955

ROME
BEYOND THE IMPERIAL
FRONTIERS

ROMAN EMPIRE IN THE
2ND CENTURY A.D. (*BLACK*)
AND ASIAN TRADE-ROUTES

Fig. 1

CHAPTER ONE

INTRODUCTION

THIS book is concerned with Roman adventuring beyond the outermost boundaries of the Roman Empire. The subject is not new; its literature indeed, both ancient and modern, is immense; but there are new examples of it, and old material has recently been reviewed. In this adventuring Greek and Arab enterprise are wedded to the Roman faculty for exploitation. The boundaries of the Empire, particularly in the East, were sufficiently fluid to ensure a constant awareness of more distant horizons, of greater riches, more marvels, fresh menaces. A century and a quarter before Trajan's thrust to the further bank of the Tigris, Maecenas at Rome, as Horace tells us, was 'fearing what the Seres [Chinese or Central Asians] may be plotting, and Bactra once ruled by Cyrus, and the discordant tribes on the banks of Tanais [Jaxartes]'. Nor was this a merely academic fear. 'The credit of the Roman money-market', said Cicero, 'is intimately bound up with the prosperity of Asia. A disaster cannot occur there without shaking our credit to its foundations.' The term 'Asia' had to Cicero a very limited implication, but the dictum was broadly true. On the European frontiers the commercial element was, from the Roman standpoint, less insistent; nevertheless, unconquered Germany remained a recurrent source of anxiety or, at its mildest, a stimulus to Roman interest and curiosity.

At the outset the word 'Roman' requires definition. It is not indeed closely definable, particularly when applied to trade. The Italian was no great sailor, just as he was no great horseman, and not a little of the trafficking beyond the frontiers involved the use of ships. Therein both fo'c'sle

and quarterdeck must, more often than not, have been
manned by Frisians, Greeks, Levantines, Arabs and others
who, like Kipling's Parnesius, had 'never seen Rome except
in a picture'. For the present purpose all these folk will pass
muster as 'Romans', so be it that they were directly in the service of Imperial commerce. There shall be no great pedantry
here in the matter of race or colour or even citizenship.

And as to geography, the widest Imperial limits of the
second century A.D. are assumed as our base-line (fig. 1).
Else, for example, we had need to remind the reader of
the Roman traders who in the first cenruries B.C. and A.D.
preceded the flag in Gallia Comata or Belgic Britain, with
tiresome argument as to Cunobelin's foreign moneyers
and the extent of his own part in the cross-Channel trade
that littered his squalid huts at Colchester with fine Arretine
dishes or brought silver goblets to pre-Claudian Welwyn.

Nor are we concerned here with the sporadic pervasion
of goods from Roman Britain into the outlands of Scotland or Ireland. Scraps of pottery and occasionally more
spectacular wares reached the native homesteads of Scotland,[1] and are there useful mainly for dating undemonstrative
local cultures. A more restricted scatter in Ireland occasionally has a similar use; as at Tara, where Professor Sean
Ó Ríordáin has dug up sherds of third-century Roman
vessels, brought by traders or (more likely) raiders to this
famous seat of kings.[2]

The bulk of our matter falls into two zones, the Euro-

1. For an account of these strays, as known in 1932, see J. Curle,
'An Inventory of Objects of Roman and Provincial Roman Origin
found on Sites in Scotland not definitely associated with Roman
Constructions', *Proceedings of the Society of Antiquaries of Scotland*,
LXVI (1932), 277–397.

2. For Roman goods found in Ireland prior to 1948, see S. P.
Ó Ríordáin in *Proceedings of the Royal Irish Academy* (Section C),
LI (1948), 35–82. The sherds from Tara were found in 1952–3.

pean and the Asiatic. A third is beginning to emerge in the deserts of North Africa, where there is accumulating evidence that the traders who brought ivory northwards across the Sahara to the coastal cities of Libya carried back Roman goods far into the interior; and though this fact may not be one of far-reaching historical significance, the importations have at least a value archaeologically as a potential means of dating associated African cultures. The East African coast, another likely region for Roman contacts, is at present virtually unexplored.

Our evidence in the following pages will be of two main kinds. First there are extensive and largely familiar references to this trans-frontier venturing in the classical and Asian records. Secondly, there are numerous discoveries of Roman or Graeco-Roman commodities, or of native goods reflecting classical influences, in lands without the Empire. Most, though not all, of the literary references have a commercial context. The material 'finds', whether in Free Germany or in further Asia, are often more difficult to interpret. A majority of them, especially in India or Indo-China, are manifestly the products of trade or at least of commercial drift. A minority may be explained as the fruits of war; as when the three legions under Varus were overwhelmed by the German tribesmen in A.D. 9 and lost their whole vast equipment to the victors. Other objects of value found their way across the borders as propitiatory gifts to native princes; as in our own time golden sovereigns, for example, have flowed diplomatically into Arabia. Again, tribal movement across or along the frontiers of Central Europe must have involved a displacement of Roman things on a fairly considerable scale. By and large, the problem of interpretation is not a simple one. It must be discussed at later stages in the light of individual circumstance.

But, when all is said, trade will be discovered as the dominant factor in these remote contacts. The Roman traders and their agents were venturesome folk, whether we regard the enterprising knight who in the time of Nero made his way to the Baltic and brought back a great load of amber, or the pioneers who in the 2nd century reopened the trans-Asian 'Silk Route' beyond Tashkurgan, or again those others who in A.D. 166 carried gifts to the emperor of China and so opened or reopened a sea-way to the Far East. Amber, pearls, pepper, silk, such were the goals of all this trafficking, and most of it is of interest to us to-day in the sense that perilous voyaging and travellers' tales are of perennial interest to those who care for human enterprise. But once at least this trafficking did something more than merely scatter Roman bric-à-brac across the world. In Afghanistan and what is now West Pakistan it was the instrument of a cultural contact which had a far-reaching effect upon the history of art.

It stands to reason that the surviving vestiges of this interchange are in kind but a fraction of the whole, and that their survival is fraught with all manner of accident. The slaves, and hunting-dogs, and corn imported into the Roman world from Britain; the cotton cloth from India; the wine that flowed into Free Germany or was borne by the monsoon to the tables of Indian princes; the 'Seric' skins from High Asia, the silk from China; the spice that filled the Pepper Barns of Rome; for these and much else we have to rely almost entirely upon chance scraps of history. In the circumstances, the surprising thing is not how little but how much has survived in the form of material evidence. Roman coinage reached India in quantity and even penetrated to Indo-China. Roman glass has been recorded from the Trondheim fiord on the one hand and (admittedly with less certainty) from Honan and Korea on the other. Silver cups from Italy and the provinces equipped the graves of the native nobility in Germany, Czechoslovakia, Poland, and Denmark. Bronze vessels reached Norway and western India. To western India again, and to Afghanistan, came Roman bronze figurines, and others have been recovered from the native homestead-mounds of the Low Countries. Red-glazed pottery from Italy or the western provinces is found alike in Poland and on the Coromandel Coast. Roman arms and armour were dedicated in the meres of Jutland. The list might be extended, and will in due course be dealt with categorically. Meanwhile, enough has been said to indicate its range.

From this point, the book will be divided into three parts, dealing respectively with Europe, Africa, and Asia. Europe will for our purpose comprise Free Germany (including Scandinavia); Africa will be subdivided into the Sahara and the East Coast; Asia will include the Indo-Pakistan sub-continent and Afghanistan on the one hand, and the Far East on the other. Two important regions are omitted: Russia, and the variable eastern frontier with Persia. For both, much further ground-work is needed. The latter in particular, with its rich historical background and the incessant military, political, and cultural interaction which, for example, brought Mithraism and Manichaeism to Europe and immortalized the ignominy of three Roman emperors on the crags of Bishapur and Naqsh-i-Rustam[1] now demands a particular and extensive study beyond the scope of the present book. Such study, when undertaken, will produce a strange *mélange* of thought and form, including incidentally a surprising manifestation of Celtic art from the Rhineland in 3rd-century Dura beside the Euphrates. But whether the long-range traffic which

1. B. C. MacDermot, 'Roman emperors in the Sassanian reliefs', *Journ. of Roman Studies*, XLIV (1954), 76.

contributed to the prosperity of Palmyra and her satellite ports on the Persian Gulf ever approached in significance that of Alexandria, of which something will be said in a later chapter, seems increasingly doubtful. Judgement must remain open pending the fuller evaluation of work such as that now in progress at Hatra and, above all, a comprehensive publication of the material from Palmyra itself.

PART ONE: EUROPE

CHAPTER TWO

FREE GERMANY:
THE LITERARY EVIDENCE

BEFORE the middle of the first century B.C. hardy Roman business-men were already operating amidst the German tribes across the Rhine. 'The Suebi', Caesar tells us (*De Bello Gallico*, IV, 1–3), 'by far the largest and most warlike nation amongst the Germans, give access to traders, rather to secure buyers for what they have captured in war than to satisfy any craving for imports.' The Suebi were an amalgam of German tribes who, in the time of Strabo (late first century B.C.) were living between the Rhine and the Elbe, and in that of Tacitus, about A.D. 98, were occupying 'more than half Germany'; more precisely, north-western Germany and the middle and lower Rhine as far as the sea. Caesar adds that 'they suffer no importation of wine what-soever, believing that men are thereby rendered too soft and womanish for the endurance of hardship'. This re-mark implies that elsewhere wine was an acceptable import; Tacitus (*Germania*, 23) states that 'the Germans who live nearest the Rhine can actually get wine in the market', whilst those in the interior 'extract a juice from barley or grain, which is fermented to make something not unlike wine'. Roman wine-vessels from the Jutland Peninsula are found to have contained a fermented drink made from malt and berry-juice, recalling the cranberry wine, mixed with myrtle and honey, of which desiccated remains are found already in Danish burials of the Bronze Age, over

1,000 years earlier. Caesar does not tell us what the Roman traders gave in exchange for surplus Suebian loot, but it may be supposed that silver money and Roman metalwork formed, now as later, a part of the apparatus.

Certainly by the first century A.D. Roman silver coinage was an established factor in the German trade. Again Tacitus is our historian (*Germ.* 5): 'The Germans nearest us value gold and silver for their use in trade, and recognize and prefer certain types of Roman money. (The peoples of the interior, truer to the plain old ways, employ barter.) They like money that is old and familiar, *denarii* with the notched edge and the type of two-horse chariot. Another point is that they try to get silver in preference to gold. They have no predilection for the metal, but find plenty of silver change more serviceable in buying cheap and common goods.' The distribution-map (fig. 7, p. 87) shows that by the third century Roman coinage had spread into Germany far beyond the vicinity of the *limes*. The preference for the older types of silver obviously derives from the dilution of the *denarius* by Nero, and reflects the native use of the money, not as a token currency backed by a state guarantee (for there could be none such beyond the frontier), but as so much bullion of honest intrinsic worth. That intrinsic worth was permanently impaired by the monetary 'reform' of A.D. 63. More will be said of this matter in a later chapter (p. 83).

The early trade across the frontiers was not without its dangers to the adventurers who undertook it. Some thirty years after Caesar's casual reference to Roman traders amongst the Suebi, the legate of Augustus 'took vengeance on certain Celts [i.e. Germans] because they had arrested and slain Romans who entered their country to trade with them' (Dio, LIII, 26). Such vicissitudes were doubtless a part of the day's work. On the whole, however, it is to be assumed that this trafficking was welcome enough on both sides. Thus in A.D. 18, as Tacitus tells us (*Annals*, II, 62), there were domiciled at the capital of the king of the Marcomanni, i.e. in Bohemia, a number of sutlers and traders 'implanted first on foreign soil by commercial privileges, then by the lure of increased profits, and finally by oblivion of their country'. The king, Maroboduus, had himself been to Italy in his earlier days and doubtless encouraged this trade as a matter of policy and as a demonstration of enlightenment. Tacitus is reinforced by the distribution-maps (e.g. fig. 8, p. 94), which show in the earlier part of the first century, but rarely afterwards, a concentration of Roman relics in the Marcomannian area. This area was approached most readily from the neighbouring 'amber route', which left the Danube at Carnuntum and penetrated up the tributary valley of the March towards the German plain and the Baltic.

The route to the Baltic is itself the subject of a well-known episode recounted by Pliny (*Natural History*, XXXVII, 45). In the time of Nero a Roman knight, agent of a certain Julianus, made the arduous journey to the Baltic coast, where he visited *commercia* or agencies, and eventually returned, presumably by way of East Prussia and Poland, with a great quantity of amber. The pioneering character of this journey implies that previously the northern sectors of the amber traffic had been in unrestricted native hands, and the knight, though primarily concerned, it seems, with the equipment of gladiatorial shows for Nero, may well have been prospecting incidentally with a view to simplifying the trade and reducing its costs. We would give much for a sight of his report.

Commercial enterprise was not all one way. Tacitus (*Germ.* 41) states that the tribe of the Hermunduri, who lay to the north of the upper Danube as far as Thuringia, 'are the only Germans who trade with us, not only on the river-bank, but deep inside our lines, in the brilliant colony that is the capital of Raetia. They come over where they will, and without a guard. To other nations we only show off our arms and our camps; to them we expose our palaces and our country-mansions – and they do not covet them.' Free trade of this kind may not in fact have been quite as rare as Tacitus affirms. Much later, after the defeat of the insurgent Marcomanni in A.D. 173, Marcus Aurelius 'established the places and the days for their trading, for these had not been previously fixed' (Dio, LXXII, 15). Whatever the custom on the Rhine, traffic across the Danube frontier would appear to have been substantially unregulated until the disturbances of the latter half of the second century.

Trade apart, Roman things reached Germany through war and through diplomacy. For the latter two references from the *Germania* (5 and 42) are in point: 'One may see among them [the Germans] silver vessels which have been given as presents to their envoys and chiefs'; and again, 'the might and power of the kings [of the Marcomanni and the Quadi] depend upon the authority of Rome. These kings occasionally receive our armed assistance, more often our financial, and it is equally effective'. It may be assumed indeed that diplomatic bribery was a normal feature of the relationships between Rome and Free Germany, and helped very materially in the scattering of coinage and other valuables. Thus when, about A.D. 90, Chariomerus, pro-Roman king of the Cherusci, was driven from his kingdom by the Chatti, he appealed to Domitian and 'did not secure any military aid but received money' (Dio, LXVII, 5). And Decebalus, king of the Dacians, was bought off both by lavish payments and also by the receipt of technical aid. About A.D. 89 Domitian sought to keep him quiet by (sending 'large sums of money and artisans of every trade, both peaceful and warlike, and promised to keep on giving large sums in future' (Dio, LXVII, 7). This subvention was continued for ten years or more, and one of the reasons for Trajan's campaign against the Dacians was his anxiety 'at the amount of money they were receiving annually' (Dio, LXVIII, 15). The submission of the Dacian king in A.D. 102 included the surrender of his 'arms, engines and engine-makers' (Dio, LXVIII, 9), presumably the Roman technicians seconded to him by Domitian. But the flow of coinage across the frontier increased rather than diminished as time went on. The Roman gold which was freely distributed in barbarian Europe in the time of the Goths and, above all, the Huns reflects in part the continuance of this policy on an exaggerated scale at the lower limit of our period.

CHAPTER THREE

FREE GERMANY:
ROUTES AND MARKETS

BEFORE we pass from the historical to the material evidence for this interchange, something may be said of the principal areas and routes with which our study is concerned. To do this at so early a stage is of course to reverse the logical sequence, and to anticipate the map-patterns which are found to emerge from the inquiry. But the active work of Scandinavian and German scholars during the past few decades has rendered this inverted procedure possible, and it is justifiable on the ground that a summary survey such as the present is more readily intelligible if the geographical aspects are sketched in at the outset.

First let it be said that no special attention is given here to the occurrence of Roman things within a belt fifty miles wide outside the formal frontier or *limes*. A marginal spread of this kind speaks for itself and can here be simultaneously defined and dismissed. In the time of Hadrian, the frontier on which it was based extended up the Rhine nearly to Coblenz, then bore eastwards in a great salient round the Taunus, southwards into Württemberg, and eastwards again to the Danube above Regensburg. Thence it followed the Danube to the Black Sea, save where it bent northwards to the Carpathians to enclose the province of Dacia. This broad frontier-zone across Europe frames on the south and west the Free Germany with which the present chapter deals. In the north and east, that Germany is regarded as extending to Norway, Sweden, Latvia, Poland, and South Russia, without any attempted discrimination of racial and linguistic boundaries, which must indeed have been numerous and sometimes formidable. The whole vast region was an *officina gentium*, a welter of nations increasingly mobile as the Imperial era wore on, already sufficiently kaleidoscopic before the mongoloid Huns brought final chaos into it at the end of the fourth century. In the circumstances it need scarcely be emphasized that the term 'free' is here merely a euphemism for 'outside the formal boundaries of the Roman Empire in the second century A.D.', i.e. the boundaries defined above, always with the reservation that those boundaries were extensively withdrawn by the rupture of the Rhine-Danube *limes* in A.D. 258–260 and the surrender of Dacia beyond the Danube a dozen years later.

ROUTES

Far beyond the range of mere frontier-diffusion a number of main routes carried goods to and from the depths of this Free Germany (fig. 2), and the arterial traffic was supplemented by lateral pervasions which tend to blur the map-pattern and complicate its interpretation. Within the Empire the traffic was focussed on three great regions: Italy, Gaul with the German provinces, and the periphery of the Black Sea. Of these, the first to dominate the scene was naturally Italy; but in the second century A.D. the developing industries of Gaul and the Rhineland were of increasing importance, and in the third century probably outstripped Italy in their trans-frontier influence. Shortly after the middle of that century, the tribal confederacy known as the Goths, who had long been moving southwards from their Baltic homeland, encompassed the northern and western shores of the Black Sea and now became an instrument in the diffusion of the rich craftsmanship of Byzantium, South Russia, and the Near East towards barbarian Europe. Trade, conquest, subvention, drift, all contributed to the complex process of dispersal and are

Fig. 2. Principal European trade-routes

usually hard to discriminate. But in one way and another, by the third and fourth centuries Gaul and the lands of the Black Sea had between them largely replaced Italy as the sources of classical craftsmanship in Free Germany, whilst subsequently the Eastern Empire of Byzantium became the major factor. Of all this complex trade and movement through four centuries, the principal lines of intercourse and the principal termini are tolerably clear; only the motives and occasions are, more often than not, held from us.

From Italy in the first two centuries A.D. came, above all, bronze wares and glass. Of both, Campania was probably the foremost producer, although the accidental preponderance of material from the Campanian cities of Herculaneum and Pompeii tends to distort our perspective. At any rate, Aquileia at the head of the Adriatic was the chief point of assembly; it was inevitably Aquileia, for instance, that became the goal of the insurgent Marcomanni and their allies when they burst through the Julian Alps in A.D. 167. No doubt the tribesmen followed well-trodden trade-routes between the Danube and Aquileia, in particular the high-road built by Augustus through the province of Noricum (Austria) and Upper Pannonia to the Danubian fortress of Carnuntum, placed strategically at the junction with the March below Vienna. Noricum itself developed metal industries with local characters which can be recognized in graves far away in Jutland, and was clearly not blind to the strategic possibilities of its position.

From Carnuntum an early route led northwards up the valley of the March, forking westwards into Bohemia or continuing northwards through the Moravian Gates into the German plain. There it struck the upper reaches of the Oder, but soon branched northwards again towards Kalisz in western Poland and so reached the lower Vistula and the Amber Coast of the Baltic, which was its main objective. Traffic along this ancient route – indeed, long-distance traffic of the kind in any part of Free Germany – must have been a matter of constant relay with accumulating dues, and it has been suggested above that the exploratory journey of the knight of Julianus in Nero's reign was in part an attempt to simplify and cheapen the process. By whatever means, throughout the period with which we are dealing Roman things circulated fairly constantly through this natural artery from the lands tapped by the Danube if not always from Italy itself. Roman coins of the second century reached the lips of the dead in the neighbourhood of Königsberg, bronze vessels of the second and third centuries were entombed in the lands south and west of Danzig Bay, and in the fourth and fifth centuries Roman gold bestrewed the Amber Coast and the Swedish islands as token of the new, uneasy partnership of barbarism with the civilized world.

The western branch-route from the March into Bohemia had only an intermittent importance, but was more instrumental than any other known route in opening up central Europe to Roman trade in the early days of the Empire. The historical position of Bohemia, home of the powerful Marcomanni and their neighbours the Quadi, is sufficiently outstanding to demand a short historical excursus at a later stage. Meanwhile, it will suffice to observe that in the early decades of the first century A.D. Bohemia was a leading entrepôt of Roman trade in Free Germany and must have been instrumental in the diffusion of Roman goods northwards into Prussia and beyond; that by the middle of the century this trade had diminished to vanishing point; but that some sort of revival took place under the later Empire, when coinage and bronze-wares again reached the region in modest quantities. Bohemia and Silesia contain natural resources, notably tin, of value to the classical world, but the independent spirit of the local tribesmen in their secluded and forested highland homes was an obstruction to regular interchange.

Another approach into and through Bohemia from the

Danube valley lay from the vicinity of Linz across to the
Moldau and via Prague, Dresden, Meissen, Leipzig, and
Halle to the Elbe, the German Plain, the Jutland peninsula,
and Scandinavia. The route was, in part at any rate, an old
one, but as a whole its importance in the Roman period
appears to represent a secondary development and never
to have rivalled that of more easterly and more westerly
alternatives.

In the west, sea-routes and land-routes combined to
supply western Germany and the Baltic lands. The sea-
routes are necessarily less sensitive to archaeological recog-
nition but must not on that account be underrated. In the
proud record of Augustus at Ankara it is proclaimed that
'My fleet made an ocean voyage from the mouth of the
Rhine to the eastward as far as the boundaries of the Cimbri
whither before that time no Roman had penetrated either
by land or by sea; and the Cimbri, the Charydes, the
Semnones, and other German peoples of that same region
sent emissaries to seek my friendship and that of the Roman
People'. These were tribes of the Elbe valley and the Jutland peninsula, though whether the fleet circumnavigated
the peninsula on this occasion may be doubted. The
Romans were timid sailors, and it may be supposed that
the longshore tribes, above all the Frisians of the Dutch
coast, became the principal carriers of the subsequent sea-
borne trade hereabouts. Their main markets towards the
north-east lay in Jutland, where amber was procurable,
and in the populous Danish islands; and a short land-route
across the base of the peninsula between the North Sea
and the western Baltic may be presumed. Trans-peninsular
routes were a normal substitute for circumnavigation in
ancient times, and a more ambitious example within the
first century A.D. will emerge when we review the evidence
from South India (p. 172).

By land, the eastern tributaries of the Rhine offered access from the Roman frontier to Westphalia and Thuringia. The Lippe, with the fortress of Vetera (Xanten) at its base, the Ruhr from Asciburgium, less certainly the Sieg from Bonn, all played some part in this traffic; above all, perhaps the Lahn and the Main, the latter overlooked by the key-fortress at Mainz. These valley-routes tended to converge upon Paderborn in eastern Westphalia and the Weser-crossings at Minden, Hameln, and Höxter, whence dispersal into the broad lowlands towards the Elbe and even to the Baltic was not difficult.

South of Mainz the country east of the frontier becomes more broken and rugged, and clear traces of arterial traffic cease. Nevertheless, the province of Raetia, overlapping the upper waters of the Danube, must have acted in some measure as a link between Upper Germany and Gaul on the one hand and the Danubian axis on the other, and there are hints that pottery (*terra sigillata* and 'Rhenish' ware) and other objects from western factories occasionally passed this way. But the main commercial activity of Raetia was directed historically towards the north. There in the first century A.D. lay the considerable nation of the Hermunduri, whose whereabouts at various periods has given rise to considerable argument[1] and doubtless, indeed, fluctuated with the characteristic mobility of the German tribesmen. They are strangely ignored by the geographer Ptolemy about A.D. 150, but were placed by Strabo (end of the first century B.C.) east of the Elbe. On the other hand, between 7 and 3 B.C. Ahenobarbus, commander on the upper Danube, had penetrated as far as the Elbe or the Saale and, in doing so, had (according to Dio, LV, 10a) 'intercepted the Hermunduri, a tribe which for some reason or other had left their own land and were wandering

1. Reviewed in *Germania*, XXIII (1939), 262ff.

about in search of another'. He settled them on territory vacated by the Marcomanni when they moved from the neighbourhood of the Main and the Neckar to Bohemia (see below, p. 35). The name of the Hermunduri has been connected philologically with Thuringia, but, though they appear to have occupied that region during some part of their history, the identification cannot be sustained. Tacitus, as we have seen, places them nearly a hundred miles further south, describing them as 'the only Germans who trade with us . . . deep inside our lines, in the brilliant colony that is the capital of Raetia' (p. 24). We may perhaps recognize a northern and a southern branch of the tribe, one in Thuringia and the Saale-Elbe valley, the other, presumably coterminous, in Bavaria round about Nuremberg. Archaeology emphasizes the commercial importance of Thuringia, beside a traditional route between the Baltic and the west, but offers no clear illustration of the statement of Tacitus in regard to Raetia. Its reticence in this matter is a sufficient reminder of the incompleteness of our picture in times or regions where history fails us.

If we turn eastwards again, to modern Hungary or ancient Dacia and as far east as South Russia and the environs of the Black Sea, we find ourselves in lands which have been inadequately explored and are at the present time inaccessible. East of Budapest the valley of the Theiss marked a route northwards from the Danube to the Carpathian passes and so into Galicia and central Poland and on to the Baltic – a route which may be supposed to have shared in the amber trade but can scarcely have depended wholly upon it. Then, still further east, the rich environs of the Black Sea, important to us in the later third and fourth centuries, were tapped by the valleys of the Dniester and the Dnieper, the former pointing to Galicia and the Vistula or the Oder, the latter to White Russia and the

B

south-eastern Baltic. There can be little doubt that with ampler knowledge these eastern routes would be found to rival the better-known arteries of the west; the heavy distribution-pattern of fourth- and fifth-century finds, mostly from the Eastern Empire, on the Swedish islands and the East Prussian coast is sufficiently significant.

MARKETS

From routes we turn to the markets which they supplied and in doing so encounter at once the initial handicap to which reference has been made above: the vicissitudes of survival. Nevertheless, it seems likely that the principal regions of concentration on our maps are reasonably representative, if by no means complete. Of the somewhat left-handed trade which, as Caesar tells us (p. 21) the Suebi of north-western Germany encouraged in the first century B.C., there is no recognizable vestige unless certain Italic or Italo-Gaulish bronze vessels of that general period found in cremation-burials of the Weser-Elbe zone (Eggers, map 3; see Bibliography, p. 215) are attributed to it. For a majority of these vessels, however, an approach from the south-east via the upper valley of the Oder is more likely. On the other hand, Bohemia, land of the Marcomanni and the Quadi, comes appropriately on to the map during the early decades of the first century A.D., in historical circumstances which may be recalled.

Bohemia. 'Next to the Hermunduri dwell the Naristi, followed by the Marcomanni and the Quadi. The Marcomanni are conspicuous in renown and power; they won the very land they now hold by their bravery, when they drove out the Boii. . . . The might and power of the kings depend upon the authority of Rome. These kings occasionally received our armed assistance, more often our financial, and it is equally effective.' So Tacitus (*Germ.* 42). It would appear that the Marcomanni were originally settled in the valleys of the Main and Neckar, whence in the time of Caesar they took arms with his opponent Ariovistus; but in 9 B.C. Drusus, a few weeks before his death, launched an attack upon them, with the important consequence that they migrated eastwards to the uplands of Bohemia. There in country at the same time fertile and sufficiently difficult to discourage interference from the west or south, they occupied the old home of the Boii and quickly developed into a dominant native power.

Their leader in this phase of migration and aggrandisement was the celebrated king Maroboduus, who knew Rome and may actually have served with the Roman army. His knowledge enabled him both to deal with Roman diplomacy and to apply his Roman training to the organization and defence of his own large kingdom. His strength and ambition were not underrated by his opponents. A careful and skilful policy of encirclement culminated in A.D. 4 in a threefold thrust into his country – from Mainz, from Raetia, and from Illyricum – and his last-moment escape was due only to a timely revolt in Illyricum behind the advance. The frustrate campaign ended in a treaty whereby Maroboduus was acclaimed a friend of the Roman people. But, where Rome had failed to tread, Maroboduus's fellow Germans stepped in and won the day. From the north, Bohemia is penetrated by the upper valley of the Elbe and its tributary the Moldau. Up these valleys in A.D. 18 streamed a host of rival tribes under the leadership of Arminius who, since his grim victory over Varus in A.D. 9, had been the champion of German freedom. The threat was more than even the power and prestige of Maroboduus could withstand; and when Arminius received support from an exiled Marcomannian, a certain Catualda, bringing at least diplomatic encouragement from Rome, the king himself fled to his double-dealing Roman friends, to end his days, years later, in sanctuary at Ravenna.

Tacitus, it will be recalled (p. 23), tells us that, when Catualda entered the capital of the vanquished Maroboduus, he found a number of Roman traders in residence there, operating under commercial privileges which had presumably been included in the treaty of A.D. 4. That treaty may be supposed to have regularized an existing state of affairs rather than to have initiated a new one. Roman traders, like those of ascendant powers in later ages, were ever wont to precede the flag, and the Roman training of Maroboduus must have inclined him to encourage them, with or without a formal writ. Be that as it may, Italic bronze vessels of the first half of the first century A.D. are at home in Bohemia (fig. 8, p. 94), together with a considerable coinage, mainly of silver, but including gold; and from Bohemia these imports spread northwards by the river valleys to the North Sea and the Baltic.

There is evidence that at this early period the Marcomanni played something of a creative role in the development of central European craftsmanship. Geographically and ethnically they were indeed in a favourable position to do so. Coming from the west, they were in contact with the Celtic world; they looked northwards to the German plain and Scandinavia; partially romanized Noricum (Austria) was at their doorstep; Roman agents were in their midst. They fell thus under a number of diverse stimuli and for a brief time formed a sort of cultural exchange and mart.[1] Thus certain types of brooch and belt

1. See a discussion by O. Almgren, 'Zur Bedeutung des Markomannenreiches in Böhmen für die Entwicklung der germanischen Industrie in der frühen Kaiserzeit', in *Mannus*, v (Würzburg, 1913), 255–78.

fittings, particularly with stylized animal-heads, are common to Bohemia and Noricum. On the other hand, a well-known type of brooch with two piercings or circles ('eyes') on the head of the bow – a late La Tène type which in subsequent forms was to become characteristic of the Rhineland – came in from the opposite direction, from Brandenburg, Posen, and Saxony, and was developed in Bohemia, whence it passed to the Rhine after the collapse of the Maroboduus régime. And it was seemingly in Bohemia that many of the earlier drinking-horns of this period were made, to judge from the fact that there, within a restricted territory, occur all the earliest known types of bronze fittings which are elsewhere scattered sporadically from the Rhine to Gotland. It was an established custom amongst the Germans to supply their drinking-horns with metal rims and terminals and to equip them with chains or straps for suspension; in the words of Caesar (*B.G.* VI, 28): 'They zealously collect the horns and encase the edges with silver, and then at their grandest banquets use them as drinking-cups.' Examples will be mentioned later (pp. 54, 57, 60).

After the exile of Maroboduus, Italo-Bohemian commerce rapidly deteriorated. The latest Roman gold coin from Bohemia during the first century is a solitary *aureus* of Titus (A.D. 79–81), and the general run of imports had ceased nearly half a century before that date. The consolidation of Roman authority in southern and western Europe had opened up alternative routes and markets, and the Bohemian tribes, increasingly isolated and (it may be) over-crowded, were becoming restive. An uneasy peace, interrupted momentarily at the time of Domitian's Dacian war by a firm Roman diplomacy, itself bordering upon war, ended in A.D. 167, when the Marcomannian king Ballomar led his tribesmen and allies across the Danube, defeated a Roman army, and besieged the pivotal market-town of Aquileia on the Adriatic. The Roman emperor reacted with determination; the invaders were beaten back, and in 172 Marcus Aurelius led his forces to victory against the Quadi, on the eastern flank of the Marcomanni. In the following year came the turn of the Marcomanni themselves. Their territory was occupied and a part of the population was transported.[1] Thereafter they never again so nearly threatened the safety of Rome, but they did not cease to contribute to the recurrent restlessness of the Danube frontier, and such trade as lingered on was canalized and constrained by Roman treaty.[2] Only in the latter part of the fourth century did gold coinage and bronze vessels again find their way to Bohemia in appreciable quantity, at a time when eastern Europe was in the grip of the Huns.

Thuringia. Between the Thuringian Forest and the Elbe, in a rough triangle formed by Erfurt, Leipzig, and Magdeburg and extending into the Forest, a concentration of coins, particularly of the Middle Empire, is less easy to explain. With them are vessels of bronze, pottery, and glass, the two last certainly from the west. They presumably arrived in part by the river-routes from the Rhineland (p. 32), above all perhaps by an old way from Mainz over the Wetterau, continued in and beyond Thuringia by the valleys of the Saale and the Elbe. This was, incidentally, the line of a prehistoric amber-route from Jutland to the middle Rhine; a route which, until chaos supervened in the latter half of the third century A.D., alternatively continued

1. Dio, LXXII, II, 4, refers to a revolt of Marcomanni settled at Ravenna, where, incidentally, Maroboduus had been given sanctuary over a century and a half previously (see above). After the revolt, Marcus evicted the settlers.

2. Marcus established the places and the days for their trading (for these had not been previously fixed). Dio, LXXII, 15.

south-eastwards up the Elbe to Bohemia and the Danube, and so connected Thuringia with Noricum and the eastern traffic-system. Furthermore, if the Hermunduri extended to Thuringia, we have the clear witness of Tacitus (p. 23) for active intercourse more directly with the south, with the province of Raetia. Thuringia would thus appear to have occupied something of a nodal point in European trade. It is at least certain that, in a fertile region accessible though at the same time screened by a succession of massifs and woods, the Thuringians or Hermunduri developed a liking for Roman things of which some account will be given in later sections.

The Baltic Coast and Eastern Europe. A thickening of Roman goods in the approaches to the gulf of Danzig (e.g. fig. 13, p. 104) draws attention to the geographical importance of East Prussia and its environs in the commercial and political picture of the period. Historically our information is of the scantiest, although the wealth of the Pomeranian – East-Prussian coast in amber, and the popularity of amber in the ancient world, are established facts. Pliny's reference, already cited (p. 23), to a Roman knight who, in the time of Nero, set out on an exploratory journey from Carnuntum to the Baltic coast and returned with a great quantity of amber, merely underlines familiar knowledge.

But if history fails us, archaeology has produced some significant results. The coin-evidence is particularly striking. A majority of the individual Roman coins from East Prussia have been found in graves, which have produced upwards of 559 of them (Bolin; see p. 83, footnote 3), mostly *sesterces*. By far the greatest number of the coin-graves has been found north-east of the gulf of Danzig, in the coastland between the rivers Pregel and Niemen, but they extend southwards to the old border with Poland and Russia, where their apparent cessation may be due merely to lack of research. In some graves the coins were introduced as ornaments, but in others they had been placed between the lips of the dead, the Charon's fee of the classical world. Save in Samland where more than half of the coins are earlier than A.D. 138, a large majority of them date from A.D. 138 to 180 (the accession of the emperor Commodus), and in Samland itself of four hoards of *sesterces* three end with Commodus and the fourth with Septimius Severus. The second half of the second century was evidently the optimum period.

Before conclusions are drawn from this concentration of coinage, one overriding factor must be considered: namely, the circumstances of the preservation of the coins. Be it repeated that most of them have been found in graves. The prerequisite condition is that the inhabitants of the region concerned were in the habit of including coins amongst their grave-goods. Similar coins may well have circulated just as freely amongst a neighbouring people whose funerary fashions were of a different sort. And that such was almost certainly the case has been demonstrated by Eggers with the aid of two maps of the Vistula-Baltic region (fig. 3). One map shows the coin-distribution just recounted; the other shows the distribution of Roman bronze vessels found in the graves of the same area. The one map is almost exactly the complement of the other; where the coin-burials end, the burials with bronze vessels begin. The inference is not in doubt. In fact we are confronted, not with the vagaries of Roman trade, but with those of native burial-custom. The lesson is one to bear in mind in instances where the materials for such demonstration may not be available.

To the further obvious question, What ancient frontier – cultural or political – does this change in custom reflect? there is no clear answer. The region was basic in the great

Fig. 3. Differential distribution of Roman bronze vessels
and coins

movements of Goths, Vandals, and Burgundians under the Later Empire, and, behind these movements, the frontiers of the second century are too indistinct for use. The cultural division extending southwards from the gulf of Danzig roughly along the line of the Passarge river is clear enough archaeologically, but cannot be translated into history.

In the third and fourth centuries the lands flanking the lower Vistula became the repository of certain types of bronze- and glass-ware for which an origin in south-eastern Europe is predicated. These include bronze bowls covered with curved flutings, and certain types of glass beaker of kinds not present in the Rhenish or Belgian factories. More will be said of these wares at a later stage. Meanwhile, it may be observed that their distribution in the Baltic lands is reinforced by the astonishing concentration hereabouts of gold coins, *solidi*, mostly of the Eastern Empire and of dates ranging from the end of the fourth through the fifth century. Gold had now replaced silver as the staple currency or treasure, and gold matched the taste of east-European barbarism. It lined the Baltic and flowed over into the Swedish islands and the pages of the sagas.

The new emphasis thus attached to a south-north circulation in eastern Europe is consistent with certain familiar historic trends under the Later Empire. The Goths, whose earlier home had perhaps been in that part of southern Sweden which still bears the name of Gotland or Götalund, had by the second century A.D. extended across the Baltic to the Danzig plain and its environs. At about the time when their continental neighbours, the Vandals and the Burgundians, began to thrust south-westwards to the Rhine, they themselves turned southwards, advancing in loosely integrated hordes towards the Danube, the Balkans, and the Black Sea. By the middle of the third century they had become an instant threat to the Danubian territories of the Empire. Roman armies, rallied by one emperor or another in this chaotic time, made a poor show against them, and it was not until A.D. 269 that the second Claudius earned the title 'Gothicus' by crushing them at the battle of Naissus, far down in modern Yugoslavia. Meanwhile, a host of them had made its way to the Crimea, devastated the rich cities round the shores of the Black Sea, and established a powerful Gothic kingdom there. In A.D. 276 another emperor, Tacitus, was earning the same title 'Gothicus' in an attempt to check them in the heart of Asia Minor.

This folk-wandering over vast stretches of eastern Europe and western Asia must not, however, be regarded in terms of an advancing army. Rather was it the intermittent and partial thrusting of droves, sometimes larger, sometimes smaller, from an inchoate mass of tribes and septs vaguely co-ordinated as 'Goths', but dependent largely on the accidents of individual leadership. Long after a Gothic horde had penetrated to Cilicia, other Goths were still threatening the Danubian frontier of the Empire or were even being enrolled in the Roman army; and, as every schoolboy knows, in A.D. 410 a Gothic king sacked Rome itself. In the third and fourth centuries, from the Baltic to the Danube and the Black Sea, in contact alike with Italy and the Eastern Empire, was a continuum of German peoples who may be loosely aggregated as Goths: to be complicated but not entirely broken at the end of our period (after A.D. 370) by the first incursions of the Asiatic Huns, whose depredations in and beyond the Danubian regions lie mostly outside the present story. The context was complete for that increasing circulation of Roman, and particularly East Roman, things throughout this wide, uneasy zone and turbulent period. Our bronzes and glassware of non-western types in East Prussia and the Baltic are an acceptable illustration of the process; whilst upwards of 54 hoards of late second or early third century *denarii* in Russia, containing more than 11,000 coins, and at least seventeen hoards of similar kind from Poland (over 10,000 coins)[1] probably reflect the same complex of events. Finally, the Runic alphabet which appears to have been evolved in contact with the Greek and Latin alphabets shortly before or after A.D. 200 may have been invented by the Goths[2]; it at least owed its early and widespread distribution between south-eastern Europe and Scandinavia to the constant interchange of commodities and ideas within this Gothic zone.

Jutland and the Baltic Islands. Mention has been made in the preceding section of the abundant gold coinage, mostly of the Eastern Empire, which in and after the end of the fourth century A.D. overflowed to the Prussian coast and the Swedish islands, Gotland and Oland. By the fifth century these islands were in the main stream of a vigorous if superficial intercourse between the Black Sea and the Byzantine world on the one hand and Scandinavia on the other. But in earlier times the hegemony of the Baltic lay rather with the great Danish islands – Zealand, Fyen, Laaland – which bar its outlet towards the Kattegat and the North Sea. These – indeed, all the major Baltic islands – were at the same time sufficiently large, sufficiently secluded, and yet sufficiently accessible to support effective groups of seafarers and their families under conditions of security hard to obtain on the mainland. Through-shipping must often have sought them, whether from choice or from adverse winds, and have contributed to their wealth. As bases for trade or piracy they had everything to offer. And their amenities extended to the sounds and firths of

1. T. Arne in *Oldtiden*, VII, 208.

2. Summary of views in H. Shetelig and H. Falk, *Scandinavian Archaeology* (Oxford, 1937), chap. XIII.

the Jutish peninsula, where was also a natural store of exportable amber. It is here then, at the western end of the inland sea, on island and mainland, that our maps show an early and continuing bias towards imported wares. For example, of more than 500 Roman vessels of bronze and 300 of glass known from Scandinavia, a great majority come from Denmark.

Land- and sea-routes, sources in the south-east and in the south-west, alike contributed to this concentration. At one time or another in the first four centuries A.D. Denmark drew its exotic wealth down the Oder and the Elbe from central and southern Europe, and by the North Sea coast from Gaul. The first check came with the great tribal movements which broke the Rhine-Danube frontier of the Empire in A.D. 258-60. Coin-evidence suggests that from that time the Elbe route, hitherto fostered by the Thuringians or Hermunduri beside its middle reaches (p. 38) ceased to play any important part in the business. And though goods from the Roman world continued in one way and another to reach Denmark throughout the fourth century, the main axis thereafter swung eastwards to the Swedish islands and the Pomeranian – East-Prussian sea-board, which has been well described as one long quay at this period, busiest at its eastern end about the delta of the Vistula.

The cultural unity and uniform wealth of Jutland and the Danish islands in the first three centuries A.D. is difficult to understand save in terms of some sort of political unity on which history is silent. A West Baltic kingdom with a sphere of influence extending to the mainland on the west and south would explain the attractiveness of this region to North Sea and continental traffic, and would make sense of our distribution-maps (e.g. fig. 9, p. 97). It is tempting to suppose that something of the old spirit of the Cimbri, who had ravaged western Europe at the end of the second century B.C., survived here in the neighbourhood of their original peninsular home, and possibly derived a new force from the compression imposed by the Imperial frontier. On the other hand, a closer analysis of the Danish evidence has suggested that this inferred West Baltic kingdom may have been centred primarily, not on the Jutish or Cimbric peninsula, but rather on the neighbouring islands, and that it spread thence to the mainland at a relatively late date. About A.D. 200 a break has been observed in the native culture of Jutland.[1] Pottery-types and brooch-forms change about that time, villages are abandoned, cemeteries discontinued. New cultural influences now come in from the islands, where the tradition remains unbroken. The evidence requires further thought, but meanwhile the picture is that of an island-kingdom of the second century A.D., with headquarters perhaps on Zealand, abruptly extending its dominion into the peninsula early in the following century and somewhat drastically remodelling the way of life there. The third century, be it added, was the heyday of the vast peat-bog deposits (p. 74), which, whatever their precise cause, sufficiently show that great things were afoot at that time.

Then in the eastern Baltic we seem to have in the time of the Later Empire a successor state or federation to this western kingdom at a time when Goths from southern Sweden and Burgundians from Bornholm had started upon their continental ventures, incidentally unifying the east Baltic coastlands and islands, and transforming them in effect into a sort of 'Gothic base'. Any more precise definition of the political situation in the two Baltic zones would exceed the evidence, but such at least is the trend of the archaeological distributions.

1. H. Norling-Christensen in *Acta Archaeologica*, XIV (1943), 138.

Norway and Sweden. Save for the Swedish islands (in particular Gotland), Norway and Sweden may be described as the 'poor relations' of Europe in the first and second centuries A.D. In contrast to Denmark, their distribution maps are significantly thin until the great continental disturbances of the third and fourth centuries gave a new value to these peripheral regions as refuges and bases. Not a single silver cup of the type well represented in Denmark and northern Germany found its way across the Baltic. Of the 'chieftains' burials' which have provided a rich harvest of Roman objects on the mainland, only one poverty-stricken example is known from the Scandinavian peninsula. Even the almost universal *terra sigillata* is absent there, except for a single example from Gotland (fig. 14, p. 110). A trickle of Roman goods penetrated to the Oslo, Stavanger, and Trondheim fiords and to the lowlands behind Stockholm, and bronze vessels of the plainest and cheapest type occur there (fig. 10, p. 98). But only when cut-glass vessels or rilled bronze bowls of the Later Empire, or glass drinking-horns of the fourth-fifth centuries, began to circulate did the fringe of Norway – in so far as a resistant geography permitted – attract imports of the better class. The principal interest of these late distributions is that they reflect a new coastwise liveliness and herald the era of the great North Sea folk-wanderings.

CHAPTER FOUR

CIRCUMSTANCES OF DISCOVERY

GRAVES, settlement-sites, peat-bogs, undefined deposits have all contributed to the very considerable bulk of Roman material now available from Free Germany. In his recent lists, which exclude coins, brooches, and beads, Eggers[1] has catalogued no fewer than 2,257 find-spots, some of which have produced a considerable array of objects. Nevertheless, the limitations of this material are worth a moment's thought at the outset, for its recovery has been subject to many distorting conditions. Thus, Denmark and the Netherlands have been more systematically explored than most other regions, and, in particular, the mass of find-spots along the Dutch coast is due largely to this cause. Large areas, on the other hand, such as Poland, which should produce much, have been underworked. Outside Holland, few native settlements of the time of the Empire have been excavated beyond the *limes* or frontier. Graves, though better-recorded, are very liable to be arbitrary in their representation. Rich burials such as the so-called 'chieftains' graves' probably overweight the areas in which they happen to occur. On the other hand the cremation-burials which represent the normal German rite generally contain few grave-goods. Burial customs in one region may specialize in the deposition of coins, in another that of bronze *situlae*, without any necessarily exact relationship to the respective distributions of those objects amongst the contemporary living. Even in a rich cremation-burial, associated objects may have become unrecognizable through burning. Peat-bog dedications, again, are restricted to the distribution of ancient

1. See Bibliography, p. 215.

marshes or meres; moreover, their discovery is necessarily more fortuitous than that of burials which, even if not marked by mounds, commonly occur in groups or cemeteries. Finally, in assessing the evidence after it has been marshalled, how are we to interpret differences of burial custom? – as indices of social stratification? of chronology? of tribal distribution? Does a continuous, linear distribution reflect a trade-route, a campaign, a migration? Or is it simply a natural zone of occupation? And what, in any particular instance, is the significance of a blank space on the map? Is it merely an accidental gap in knowledge? If not, what is its probable meaning? These are some of the questions which may fairly be asked – and must often enough remain unanswered.

Burials are by far the most productive source of evidence, and amongst them priority must be given to a remarkable group of inhumations which, in spite of an approximate uniformity, are widely spread in place and time.

(*a*) *Chieftains' graves of the Lübsow group*, so named from their richness and from the occurrence of five of them at Lübsow, between Stettin and Kolberg in Pomerania. They extend from the upper waters of the Oder in the south-east across the German Plain to Fyen and Danish Slesvig in the north-west, with a solitary poor relation in Norway, at Storedal near Oslo (fig. 4, p. 50). Their limit towards the west is marked by two examples between the Elbe and the Weser. Of the thirty-two burials recorded,[1] all save two or three are inhumations. The graves are sometimes covered by a mound, but are generally devoid of surviving surface-indication, and the dead were often, perhaps always, placed in wooden coffins. The wealth of their equipment, and the exotic character of much of it, relegate them to a class by themselves. Roman imports include banqueting

1. Eggers, p. 50.

services consisting of cups of silver or glass, bronze wine-
buckets, dishes, jugs, ladles, strainers and 'saucepans', together with toilet objects such as mirrors and combs;
whilst among native products are silver or bronze brooches,

Fig. 4. Map showing 'Chieftains' Graves' of the Lübsow Group

ornamented hair-pins, gold finger-rings, silver and bronze buckles and other belt-fittings, gold-filigree beads, bronze knives and shears, dice and gaming-pieces, drinking-horns fitted with silver and bronze, casket-fittings, pottery, and sometimes spurs, but, be it noted, never weapons. Joints of meat were also placed in the graves, together with a fermented drink made – as traces in the wine-vessels show – from barley and local berries. ('For drink', says Tacitus, *Germ.* 23, 'they extract a juice from barley or grain.') Men and women were buried with equal pomp, as befits the honourable status ascribed to German women by Tacitus.

Inhumation was not the German Iron Age custom, and its prevalence in the chieftain-burials has been ascribed, like many of their contents, to the new contact with Roman culture. The explanations is invalid, since at the time of a majority of these burials, the normal Roman custom was cremation. We are left with a puzzling paradox. For 1,000 years cremation had been the rule in Germany and Scandinavia. Only when we reach back beyond a rather shabby and reluctant Early Iron Age to the glorious Scandinavian Early Bronze Age do we find northern rites comparable with those of the Lübsow group: the dead buried unburnt with their cherished possessions about them – armlets of gold, swords, daggers, axes, brooches, skins and textiles, cups and bowls, even sprigs of blossom. It was as though now, with the advent of new resources under the Early Empire, the 'new rich' were reviving the magnificence of their own remote past. There is nothing to suggest the arrival of a new aristocracy from without; no known tribal or national boundary defines the revolutionary mode. An inter-tribal fashion, based upon an access of wealth, had swept across central Europe in front of the organized and masterful approach of the culture of the Mediterranean. It represented the prerogative of an aristocracy or plutocracy (deriving its wealth from some now-unidentifiable source) with ideas of its own – a naïve desire to continue intact in their graves the delights of a pre-eminently peaceful and sumptuous existence. That the divergent burial custom, like the intrusive riches, characterized a limited class is in accordance with analogies from the ancient and modern world. In India, for example, certain Hindu ruling families have long inhumed their dead amidst subjects who adhere to cremation. So about the chieftains' graves of the Lübsow group the ordinary tribesman normally continued to burn his dead, humbly enough, in the traditional manner.

This sudden appearance of classical furniture in Free Germany is remarkable, but not without parallel. Much the same sort of thing had indeed happened not very long before within the Celtic fringe some three hundred miles further south. In the fifth and fourth centuries B.C. the opening up of eastern Gaul to Mediterranean trade from Massilia (Marseilles) and northern Italy had led to an influx of classical luxuries, particularly wine and table-gear, into the region dominated by wealthy Celtic aristocracies between the Rhine and the Moselle. There had ensued in these parts new standards of good living in what passed for the civilized Mediterranean mode, with all the prestige of 'Etruscan' wine-jars, Greek cups, and bizarre imitations of them. No cultural connexion need or can be sought between these Celts and our Lübsow Germans; the common factor is the response of a flamboyant barbarism to sudden opportunity for exotic display and affectation.

By what route or routes the Roman imports reached these Lübsow chieftains is clear enough. Some contact from an early date with the romanized West either by land or by the North Sea cannot be precluded, but there can be no doubt that the principal approach was from Italy direct, by the Danube and the March to the systems of the Elbe and the Oder. The map-distribution and the character of the imports combine in proof, and a third factor coincides. With scarcely an exception, the imports to which a southern (mostly Italian) origin may be ascribed antedate the great war against the Marcomanni and the Quadi of Bohemia in A.D. 167–73 (above, p. 37). This war, and the prolonged disturbances of which it was a peak, must seriously have restricted trans-Alpine traffic; and it can be no mere chance that it was only then and thereafter that the Lübsow 'chieftains' or their successors turned mainly to western markets for their goods, their old sources of supply now largely closed to them.

At the same time, a source of supply other than normal long-distance trade may in some cases be suspected. Diplomatic gifts of plate to ingratiate native princes are attested by Tacitus for Germany (above, p. 24) and by the *Periplus* for the East (below, p. 142), and some of the more costly collections of classical table-ware from Free Germany may have originated in this practice. The nearest approach to direct evidence for it is supplied by the famous find from Hoby, which constitutes the most remarkable assemblage of classical metal-wares from any single spot in Free Germany, with the exception of the Hildesheim hoard and the peat-bog deposits.

In 1920 at Hoby, on the south coast of the Danish island of Laaland, a richly furnished burial was found by chance and excavated without method.[1] The general features are, however, clear. In an unmarked grave lay the skeleton of a middle-aged man with his head towards the north-east. No evidence of a coffin was observed, but on analogy it is not unlikely that one was present. Beside the dead had been buried two joints of pork and a magnificent table-service,

1. K. Friis Johansen, 'Hoby-fundet', in *Nordiska Fortidsminder*, II, Hefte 3.

mostly in the more northerly part of the grave near the head and chest of the skeleton. The equipment included a pair of decorated classical silver cups placed on a bronze tray which had been tinned internally; a plain silver cup or ladle to which a vigorous zoomorphic handle of bronze had been fitted by a non-classical craftsman; also of bronze, a *situla* or bucket, a *patera* or saucepan, a jug; two bronze-mounted drinking-horns; seven brooches of bronze or silver, one with inlaid gold; two gold finger-rings; a bronze belt-buckle; a bronze knife; a bone pin; and three clay pots. The datable objects are of the end of the first century B.C. or the beginning of the first century A.D., the time of Augustus. The burial thus constitutes probably the earliest of the known chieftains' graves of the Imperial period.

The two cups at the head of the list are cylindrical two-handled *scyphi* (a handle of one of them missing), and are finely decorated in relief in a style inherited by the academic age of Augustus from Hellenistic sculpture or painting of the fourth century B.C. One represents the visit of Priam to Achilles as recounted in the *Iliad* (pl. 2A); the other derives its subjects from the legend of Philoctetes and is probably based upon the lost *Philoctetes* of Euripides. In both, certain details of the costume and ornament are gilded. Both are signed in stippled letters by a maker named Cheirisophos, the one in Greek lettering, the other in Roman, though with the Greek form of the name. Cheirisophos was evidently a Greek craftsman, working possibly in Asia Minor, where Pliny places a centre of production, or perhaps rather in Alexandria, with an eye to the Roman market. The Philoctetes cup also bears, as these vessels often do, an indication of the total weight of the pair, and finally a graffito on the base of both gives *Silius* as the name presumably of a former owner. Two comparable *scyphi* are in the great treasure of Bosco Reale, near Pompeii, where also

the weights of important pieces and the names of owners
are inscribed. The bronze tray on which the Hoby cups
stood is of a kind more familiar to-day in the innumerable
red-glazed copies made by the Arretine potters. The jug
is of exceptional beauty, with a finely wrought frieze of
tendril-pattern and a charming little cupid at the base
of a high and graceful handle (pl. 7A). The two-handled
dish is of comparable workmanship and has a scutcheon
ornamented in relief with a figure of Venus decked by
cupids. The *situla* has a floriate handle with swan's-head
terminals and attachments adorned with cupid-masks. The
type has a wide south-east to north-west distribution across
central Europe, and even extends occasionally into Norway
and Sweden. Its Campanian origin is not in doubt, and its
bearers probably brought it via Aquileia and the Danube,
though a coastal route from the mouth of the Rhine is
possible. To a similar origin in southern Italy may be
ascribed the *patera*, which bears the maker's stamp of Cn.
Trebellius Romanus. For the rest, the contents of the grave
are of non-Roman workmanship. The pair of drinking-
horns have knobbed or 'baluster' terminals of the longer and
earlier type. Most of the brooches belong to a specifically
Danish series of the early Roman period; and, lastly, the
pottery is, as might be expected, also of local provenance.

In grave-deposits, cups and drinking-horns are found,
hospitably enough, in pairs according to an established
Roman habit,[1] though the concurrence of the two types of

1. Represented, for example, in the hoards from Bosco Reale and
the House of Menander at Pompeii, and, far away in pre-Claudian
Britain, in the two imported silver cups at Welwyn, Hertfordshire.
Chemical analysis has shown that, of a pair of native drinking-horns
of early Imperial date found in a peat-bog at Skudstrup, Kr. Haders-
leben, in Danish Slesvig, one had contained mead from honey, the
other beer from emmer-wheat. Whether the pairs of classical cups
had similarly contained different kinds of wine or were merely a

vessel – whether for different beverages or customs, or whether the foreign silver was merely an added luxury – is not explained. At any rate, Campania and Asia Minor or Alexandria had contributed lavishly to the gear of the dead man of Hoby, lying there with his clothing pinned about him by a fine array of native brooches. The question remains: How had a complete Roman drinking-service, consisting of no less than eight pieces, come to this far-off Danish island and to a single grave? By trade, it may be; but here if anywhere we have an example of the diplomatic presentation of gold and silver plate referred to by Tacitus. For it has been plausibly suggested that the 'Silius' who had owned the silver cup was none other than the C. Silius who was legate of Upper Germany from A.D. 14 to 21.

Another burial of the same general kind but a century later in date shows interesting variations in detail and is better recorded. At Dollerup, about ten miles west of Kolding in the Ribe district at the base of the Jutland peninsula, the discovery of pottery and other relics of various dates within the Roman period led in 1947 to a methodical exploration which revealed a remarkable double burial.[1] Two graves lay parallel with each other, roughly east and

symbol of hospitality is not known. The latter explanation seems unlikely. Whatever the meaning of the custom, it was represented in no less than seventeen of the 'chieftains' graves' by pairs of metal or glass drinking-vessels, and had been taken over from the Roman world with the goods themselves. When the source of supply shifted from Italy to Gaul in the latter half of the second century, cups were no longer distributed in pairs; nevertheless, their German recipients continued to observe the Italian custom and made up pairs of odd vessels. See J. Werner, 'Römische Trinkgefässe in germanischen Gräbern der Kaiserzeit', in *Ur- und Frühgeschichte als historische Wissenschaft* (E. Wahle Festschrift), ed. by H. Kirchner (Heidelberg, 1950), pp. 168-76.

1. O. Voss and M. Ørsnes-Christensen in *Acta Archaeologica*, XIX (Copenhagen, 1948), 209ff.

west, with less than one mile between them, and the symmetrical but overlapping disposition of pots upon this intervening balk seemed to indicate simultaneous burial. The bodies had been placed in oak coffins of semicircular section, preserving the contour of the tree, and had been laid out on, or shrouded in, cow-hide. The pattern of the grave-goods showed that the heads had been towards the west, although the actual bones had disappeared save for some of the teeth. The more northerly grave contained a large pottery vase near the head; an iron brooch with silver inlay and traces of cloth where the chest had been, recalling the words of Tacitus (*Germ.* 17) that 'the universal dress is the short cloak, fastened with a brooch or, failing that, a thorn'; two drinking-horns with bronze mouth-rings close to the face of the dead and, at the pointed ends, bronze caps in the form of ox-heads; adjoining these, fragments of silver hooks and bronze fittings, including a buckle; a plain gold finger-ring; two rows of ornamented silver studs; and at the foot two clay vessels – a cup and a dish – with an iron knife and indeterminate objects of iron and wood. The more southerly grave included similarly a large pottery vase near the head; a silver brooch at the base of the throat, with remains of cloth, hide, cord and a bead or pendant of silver wire; two plain gold finger-rings where the right hand had presumably been; towards the foot of the coffin, two prick-spurs of bronze with silver filigree and iron points, and two sets of three round silver filigree discs with pierced lugs for attachment, traces of silver ornaments and a blue glass bead; and, beyond these, an iron knife with remains of a silver-mounted sheath, two bronze *situlae* or buckets which may have been wrapped in cloth, two clay pots, and two silver cups which had stood upon a round wooden tray; and, lastly, fragments of a bone comb. The southern grave had evidently been that of a man, but whether the northern had been that of a woman is less certain.

Typical analysis of this varied assortment of objects, particularly of the *situlae*, brooches, spurs, and comb, indicates a date not earlier than the end of the first and more probably within the second century A.D. for the two burials. In the present context interest attaches primarily to the bronze buckets and the silver cups. The former, 25·5 cm. high, are of double-conical form (Eggers types 24–9),[1] each with three pelta-shaped feet, a pail-handle, and soldered handle-attachments bearing human masks flanked by fish-heads. Similar handle-attachments were found long ago in a mound at Højsted (Rumperup) in the Holbæk district of Denmark with a *patera* stamped by L. Ansius Epaphroditus, who worked in Campania in the latter half of the first century A.D. On the other hand, none of these double-conical *situlae* seems to be recorded from Pompeii, so that their vogue would appear to have been after A.D. 79. An example from the Bosco Reale treasure, lost at that time, is typologically earlier; and a central date about A.D. 100, with wide margins, may be ascribed to the Dollerup vessels, always with the possibility of a long life prior to burial.

The two-handled silver cups found beside them are a more difficult problem (pl. 2B). They are 7·9 cm. high, have bands of zigzag, herring-bone, and other simple linear ornamentation round the upper part of the bowl with a fringe of pendant triangles, and the disc-foot of the cup is decorated with a further band of triangles. The handles are flanked at the top (on the 'thumb-plate') by swans' heads and terminate below in a conventionalized animal head with bulbous muzzle. All the ornamentation, including the top surface of the handles, is gold-plated. The cups are of a familiar classical form of the first centuries B.C. and A.D.,

1. See Bibliography, p. 215.

but details point to provincial workmanship. The crude ornamentation both on the thumb-plates and on the body is not of the normal Mediterranean standard, and the free use of emphatic triangular or denticular motifs is indeed a feature of the local pottery from the same burial. Non-Roman features have been observed in other cups of the series (p. 54). Certainly the animal head at the base of the Dollerup handles has nothing to do with Roman art; it is comparable with the terminal heads of armlets, finger-rings, and belt-fittings over a wide zone of central Europe, extending from Jutland through north Germany to Poland and lower Austria, with a possible origin in the province of Noricum. Thus rather by a process of elimination than by compelling evidence the Dollerup cups have themselves been attributed to a factory somewhere in that gold-producing Roman province. At least it can be affirmed that, however 'barbarian' some of their characters may be, they are as unlikely at this period to have been a product of Free Germany as of metropolitan Italy. It is sufficient to recall the words of Tacitus: 'Heaven has denied them [the Germans] gold and silver – shall I say in mercy or in wrath?'

Yet a third group of burials, somewhat later in date (perhaps A.D. 150–200), may be described briefly to illustrate the range of these rich deposits. Again in the island of Laaland, at Juellinge, four graves were found in 1909, and three of them were excavated with care.[1] They were oriented north-south, and the dead – all apparently women, young and aged – had been buried in coffins, with the heads towards the north. The graves were sealed by a number of large stones, and with the coffins or in the filling above them were joints of lamb; in one case, the complete forepart of a lamb at one end and the hind-quarters at the

1. Sophus Muller, 'Juellinge-fundet', in *Nordiske Fortidsminder*, II, Hefte 1.

other. The best-preserved of the burials, now in the
National Museum at Copenhagen, may represent the series
(pls. 3 and 4). It was that of a woman who had died in her
thirties and had, incidentally, been lamed by a deformity of
her right leg. She lay on her right side with legs slightly
flexed, and had been buried with her ornaments and clothing about her: two gold-headed silver pins in her hair, an
S-shaped silver clasp with a gold pendant and two gold
beads at her neck, four silver brooches (two of them much
worn) on the chest and shoulders, two beads of amber and
glass under the right wrist, and a plain gold ring on the ring-
finger of the right hand. A mass of material under and about
the head probably represented a cushion. And held in the right
hand was a bronze wine-strainer in the form of a small bowl
pierced as a sieve at the end of a long and slender handle.

Beyond the head were the remains of a wooden box with
a bronze lock. It had been buried with the lid open, and
contained toilet implements: a bone comb, bronze shears,
a bone pin, and an S-shaped bronze knife. Beside the box
was a pair of Roman cut-glass beakers, and beside them
again the remains of a pair of drinking-horns with mounts
of partially silvered bronze. Their knobbed terminals are
of the shorter and later variety (compare above, p. 55).
Beyond the horns again was a bronze cauldron of a plain,
convex-sided classical type (Eggers type 40) relatively
common in Free Germany in the second and possibly third
centuries A.D. Although it is found also, as here, in wealthy
graves, it was essentially the 'poor man's' type, and as such
had a wide vogue in the poorer lands of the north, Sweden
and Norway. Within the cauldron, but formerly, it seems,
on a wooden tray placed over it, lay a bronze ladle into
which the strainer held by the dead fist; the two instruments
were used together in the process of ladling the drink from the
cauldron into the beakers or horns. A deposit in the bottom

of the cauldron showed on analysis that this had contained a fermented drink made from barley and fruits of the country-side, and the soot which covered the exterior of the cauldron was presumably the result of the mulling of its contents.

The gentility implied by these Juellinge burial-groups with their classical imports of bronze and glass must be tempered by the observation that it was at best of a some-what shabby kind. At any rate, by the time that they were buried, the imported bronze vessels were much worn and patched and the fact that one of them, a *patera*, bears the stamp of L. Ansius Diodorus, who worked probably at Capua both before and after the destruction of Pompeii in A.D. 79, has no close bearing upon the date of deposit. Further, at least one of the glass beakers in the grave which has been described was seemingly damaged and useless at the time of burial. Indeed, the whole aspect of the contents of the graves was that either of a decayed heritage from better times or of an economical selection of worn-out commodities, at least in respect of non-native products. All things considered, the date of the series must be well on in the second century.

Finally, it is only fair to the 'Lübsow group' to make some reference to the first of the burials found in 1908 at Lübsow itself, particularly since, unlike those described above, this may possibly have been a cremation. The dis-covery was, as often, accidental and the precise facts are uncertain,[1] but it would appear that the remains had been placed in a grave perhaps some six feet in length with paved floor, stone-built sides, and a large cover-stone, surmounted by a cairn possibly five or six feet high. At one end of the grave were clay urns containing ashes which may or may not have been human, and the lower parts of the side-walls showed evidence of fire, supposedly from

1. E. Pernice in *Prähistorische Zeitschrift*, IV (1912), 126ff.

contact with hot wood-ash brought from the funeral pyre. But in spite of the seeming intrusion of the normal German rite of cremation, the grave has all the general aspect and equipment of an inhumation-grave of 'chieftain' type. Apart from two drinking-horns, four brooches (one of gold and silver), two silver pins and bronze belt-fittings, the contents included a dozen objects of first-century date from the Roman world: two silver cups, two glass bowls, a bronze wine-bucket, jug and dish, two bronze 'saucepans' or ladles, a mirror-plate of white metal, and bronze shears and tweezers. The list closely repeats those already given, and details may mostly be omitted. It will suffice to note that the two-handled silver cups had stood upon the bronze dish, as at Hoby; and that they are of a simple and graceful pedestalled form with analogies at Bosco Reale and Hildesheim, plain save for a narrow band of gilded leaf-ornament below the rim (pl. 5A). As often, under the base of each cup is scratched its weight. The glass bowls – characteristically a pair, like the silver cups and drinking-horns – are of a familiar first-century type with vertical 'pillar mouldings' round the sides, and may well be of Campanian manufacture. The bronze bucket is a fine example of the type with 'face-attachments' for the handle, i.e. with the plate attaching the handle-loops to the rim in the form of a human head: in this instance, a female head with a palmette-ruff and flanking animals' (dogs?) heads, possibly indicating Scylla. A closely similar bucket is included in the Bosco Reale hoard prior to A.D. 79, and the type is regarded therefore as a Campanian product. It penetrated fairly freely by way of the middle Danube to the Elbe–Oder river-system and so to Denmark, with two outliers in Norway (one of them as far north as the Trondheim fiord) and three in Sweden. The larger of the two 'saucepans' or *paterae* is tinned internally and in part externally, and has an early type of handle with a semicircular piercing flanked by swans' heads (fig. 8, p. 94). This type is particularly common in Bohemia, which may well have acted as an intermediary towards the north. Like the rest of the imported bronze-work in the grave, the bucket may be ascribed to Capuan or at least to Campanian workshops.

These four examples, from Hoby, Dollerup, Juellinge, and Lübsow itself, will suffice to illustrate the remarkable character of the 'chieftains' graves of Lübsow'. The durability of many of their contents, with the patent fact that some of these had obviously been long in use before burial, complicates their chronology, but most of them are safely included in the bracket A.D. 50–150. Their distribution, from Jutland to Poland, is too diffuse to conform with any conceivable political amalgam. At the same time, their astonishing uniformity indicates something more than chance. Their furniture shows us a well-to-do society inter-tribal in scope and shaped by uniform conventions and aspirations: the possession, above all, of a drinking-service, with cups (and drinking-horns) correctly duplicated in the classical tradition, and with containers, ladles, and dishes of the orthodox Italian kind. The wine, indeed, in these northern parts had not always seen the Italian sun; the proud owner of Campanian bronze or glass or Graeco-Roman silver must often enough have prefixed his wassailing with an apology for serving the humble mead and cranberry-juice which had contented his ruder ancestors. Rome, which had imposed a new culture upon the conquered west, had simultaneously imposed a new snobbery upon the unconquered north. These mute, inglorious 'chieftains' and their wives, we may suppose, were not immune from this human frailty. But they have richly contributed to archaeology if not to history.

(*b*) *Other burials.* It may be admitted that to call the wealthy, placid Lübsow folk 'chieftains' is to conform with an archaeological convention rather than to state an ascertained or even probable fact. Nothing that we know of Teutonic chieftainship would lead us to suppose that a prince of Tacitus's Germania would venture into the hereafter without at least a token armament. It may be that contact with the Roman world had brought into being, during the effective tenure of the neighbouring Roman *limes*, a tolerably settled stratum of native 'new rich' not wholly nor even largely identical with the impulsive military aristocracy of the German tradition. If so, the seeming fact that these 'new rich' faded out when major disturbances began to alter the pattern of Free Germany in the latter part of the second century is easy to understand. A hundred years later their place was taken in central Germany by other 'chieftains', wealthy indeed, but of a more traditional kind.

These later 'chieftains' have been studied particularly in the region of the Saale and its tributaries south of Halle and Leipzig.[1] They were buried north-south in large coffins or wood-lined graves, were mostly men – young to middle-aged – dressed and spurred, with gold finger-rings and silver brooches, Roman *paterae*, bowls and dishes of bronze, native and Roman pottery, Roman glass, and with silver spear-heads or arrowheads by their side. Roman coins and the types of spur and brooch indicate dates from the end of the third century to the middle of the fourth.

In these same regions are many other humbler graves, at first cremations, later including inhumations. The suggestion of the evidence as a whole is pretty clearly that of a military aristocracy and their followers within raiding-distance of the shrinking Roman frontiers at a time when

1. W. Schulz, 'Die Skelettgräber der spätrömischen Zeit in Mitteldeutschland', in *Mannus-Bibliotek* no. 22 (Leipzig, 1922); and Schulz, *Leuna: ein germanischer Bestattungsplatz der spätrömischen Kaiserzeit* (Deutsche Akademie der Wissenschaften zu Berlin, 1953).

central Europe was seething with tribal movement and
loot was abundant.

For the rest, little need here be said of the large number
of burials, mostly cremations, which have yielded Roman
goods in other parts of Free Germany. The bulk of the
material of our study is derived from them, and their
geographical extent is remarkable. In the north they reach
the head of the Trondheim fiord in Norway and the province of Vaasa in Finland. The Danish and Swedish islands
and eastern Jutland are full of them. Further south they
clutter the environs of the great river-valleys and occur
more sparsely between them. Frequently the settlements
represented by these burials have not been identified; it
may be assumed that mostly they consisted of poor huts,
such as those described on p. 68.

A single grave-field of the third century A.D. in Hanover
will here serve to illustrate in a general way the whole vast
series. At Helzendorf, Kr. Grafschaft Hoya, in that province
were found in 1936 a number of cremation-burials which
produced a medley of Roman and native craftsmanship,[1]
the latter usefully dated by the former. Most of the graves
consisted of a hole in the ground in which a bundle of burnt
bones had been placed in a cloth wrapping. A few, however, of larger size (75–100 cm. wide and up to 85 cm. deep)
contained Roman bronze vessels with their bases set firmly
in the underlying sand. Three of these were simple buckets
of the so-called 'Hemmoor' type, a Gaulish or Rhineland
product characteristic of the third century (p. 99). In two of
them with the ashes were remains of a bone comb, and in
one the oxidized metal had preserved traces of a bedding of
leaves beneath the bones. Another grave produced a bronze
bucket or *situla* with cylindrical neck above a carinated
body and with loop-attachments in the form of a woman's

1. *Germania*, XXIII (1939), 168ff.

C

head between the fore-parts of fish. This is a late variant
of the 'face-*situla*', which occurs freely from Bohemia to
Zealand – an exception to the rule that after the middle of
the first century Bohemia withdraws into the background
as a Roman market. Presumably the convenience or attractiveness of these *situlae* as ash-containers led to a circum-
vention of the normal difficulties of trade. In the Helzendorf
example the ashes had been bedded in straw. Yet another of
the graves contained a bronze tray with vertical sides and
vine-leaf handle-loops, the loops or hooks themselves ter-
minating in panthers' heads. Within the tray were a bone
comb and clear traces of the linen bag which had contained
the burnt bones, and in the same grave was a hand-made
native pot. Other objects from the cemetery included a
number of native pots, a gold finger-ring with lapis lazuli
intaglio, and a *terra sigillata* beaker of third-century type
with barbotine decoration (Ludowici form VMg), probably
of Rhenish manufacture.

Within the purlieus of the Roman frontier the native
villagers were liable on rare occasions in the third or fourth
century to adopt the late Roman custom of inhumation.
Thus at Laisack, north of the upper Danube (Raetian)
frontier near Neuberg, was found a flat grave containing a
skeleton with three bronze arrow- or lance-heads, a silver
buckle and four pots, of which one was a black-glazed Rhenish beaker of familiar late type, inscribed [RE]PLE ('fill up') in
white slip.[1] This beaker may have wandered two or three
hundred miles from its place of manufacture, but the mode
and route of its wanderings in this period of Roman with-
drawal and spasmodic German advance can only be guessed.

(*c*) *Settlements*. Any attempt to describe the homesteads
or villages of Free Germany would exceed the scope of this
book. We are not here concerned with the social and

1. *Germania* XVIII (1934), 117ff.

economic life of the German or Scandinavian tribesmen save in so far as is necessary to an understanding of the direct or indirect impact of Roman material culture upon them. The remains of their houses accord with the remarks of Tacitus in that they show a simple architecture of timber partially smeared with clay, without masonry or tiles, and are isolated one from another perhaps partly to minimize the risk of fire. Typical examples from Denmark[1] are about fifty feet long and fifteen feet broad, with lines of wall-posts supplemented externally by walls of peat or turves, and seemingly with turf-covered or thatched roofs, the construction of which was deliberately simplified by the moderateness of their span. The entrance is in the middle of one of the long sides, and the hearth, of stones covered with clay, is more or less central, but not immediately opposite the door. A stone mortar may lie on the clay floor, and there is a tendency for sherds to accumulate round the margins. Here and there scraps of Roman pottery or metalwork, or a Roman Republican or Imperial coin, occasionally of gold, but more usually of silver, may be found, but as preserved the imported material from these simple homesteads is not comparable in quantity or quality with that in the inhumation graves further east. These long houses were intended to accommodate cattle as well as the farmer and his family, the living quarters being commonly up-wind, at the eastern end.

Sometimes the distinctive long-house plan is replaced by a smaller type, more nearly square and with only two or three posts on each side. The entrance is still central, and the hearth or hearths are on the major axis. Crofts of this kind were indeed probably normal throughout Free Germany. For example, at Wittislingen in Bavaria, on the

1. For these, see J. Brøndsted, *Danmarks Oldtid* (Copenhagen, 1940), III, 107ff. and 243ff.

banks of the Egau, a southern tributary of the Upper Danube in the old province of Raetia, a Roman building of stone was destroyed (as finds show) during the great invasion of the Alamanni in A.D. 259–60.[1] Sometime later, but within the period of the Roman Empire, German settlers occupied the site and built a group of small huts, each about twelve feet square with floor sunk one-and-a-half feet below the surface and with three wall-posts on two opposite sides. The sinking of the floor is incidentally a German habit repeated in Saxon huts both in Holland and in England.

Along the Frisian coast between the mouths of the Rhine and the Elbe, local conditions imposed variations in the layout of the homestead. The land surface hereabouts was liable to flooding, and many of the huts and byres were therefore built on extensive artificial mounds or *terps* heaped up to a height of some ten to twenty feet on the local sandy clay or alluvium. These mounds have not infrequently been absorbed to a great extent by the aggradation of the surrounding plain, but attention has been directed to them from time to time in the Dutch sector by intensive agriculture, and these discoveries have been skilfully exploited and supplemented by a society formed for the purpose under the leadership of Professor A. E. van Giffen.[2] Unfortunately, any distribution-map founded on these researches is partially falsified by the accident that the adjacent stretch in Germany, between the Dutch frontier and the Elbe, where a similar type of ancient occupation may be presumed, has been used in modern times predominantly as pasturage and remains undisturbed and unexplored.

The mounds range in date from the pre-Roman Iron Age to the Carolingian period or later, though the known

1. *Germania* xxx (1952), pp. 287ff.
2. See reports of the Vereeniging voor Terpenonderzoek from 1918 onwards; and *Germania* xx (1936), 40ff.

pre-Roman examples are rare. A single notable example
will serve to represent the sequence. North-west of
Gröningen lie large numbers of the mounds – variously
known as *Terp*, *Warf*, *Werft*, *Wurt*, or *Wierde* – in the
vicinity of existing or former streams on the flat Frisian
coastland. The summit of the largest mound is crowned
by the parish church of Ezinge, at the head of the little
town which covers the gentle south-eastern slope. Towards
the north, a considerable sector of the mound was carefully
excavated by Dr van Giffen in 1931–4, and revealed a
succession of timber farmsteads ranging in date from about
300 B.C. to A.D. 400 or later. To-day the mound is some
1,500 feet in diameter and rises at the centre about seventeen
feet above the natural soil. This height is due partly to the
accumulation of occupation-material (remains of floors
and turf-walls, posts and wattle, cattle-dung, general
debris) through the centuries, but owes much to a peri-
odical building up of the site by the deliberate addition of
clay or dung in order to maintain the superimposed homestead above a flood-level which was itself rising with the
gradual aggradation of the surrounding plain. The earliest
house (Phase VI) lay in fact on the old natural surface; but
it was succeeded by a platform which grew in height and
diameter through four subsequent phases of occupation.
By the Roman period (Phases II–III) it was eleven-and-a-
half feet high and about five hundred feet in diameter.

With the exception of the crude square hut-pits which
represent the ultimate occupation (Phase I) by intrusive
Anglo-Saxons about A.D. 400, the successive homesteads
are based throughout upon certain uniform elements.
These are of considerable interest in the general history of
the house-plan, but cannot be more than referred to here.
Briefly, they comprise oblong buildings commonly divided
into a 'nave' and two 'aisles' by internal lines of posts,

three or more in number on each side. The bays of the
aisles are sometimes partitioned into stalls, and may be
fronted along the sides of the nave by a low wickerwork
rack to carry fodder for the stalled cattle. Where the stalls
are absent, a hearth (or two hearths) in the nave indicates
human occupation. Sometimes both usages are combined
in the same building: stalls and racks towards one end and
a hearth towards the other. The whole indicates a simple

Fig. 5. Reconstruction of Early Iron Age homestead at
Ezinge, Holland

farming economy of a familiar early medieval type, here
going well back into the pre-Roman Iron Age. The buildings range in size from a small combined house and byre
thirty-one feet by 23 feet to a monstrous barn with continuous stalls and no hearth, upwards of seventy-six feet
long. The aisles (stalls) are about five feet broad. In some
instances there is a hint that the main posts may have curved
inwards as crucks. The door was placed as nearly as possible
centrally either in the end or in the side, or in both.

Each phase was marked by rebuildings which make it

difficult to establish a unitary group at any one moment. The clearest *ensemble* is included in the homestead-plan characterizing Phase v which, though approximately of the third century B.C., must closely have resembled its successors of Roman date. The main element in this *ensemble* is a large byre of the kind described, with an aisled addition to one side and flanked on the other by two smaller-aisled dwellings with hearths, and a third combined byre and dwelling. The whole makes a satisfactory reconstruction (fig. 5).

It may be added that amongst the contents of the Roman levels (Phases II–III) were bronze brooches of the first century A.D., sherds of plain and decorated *terra sigillata* of the second century, and a bronze statuette of Jupiter. Roman statuettes may indeed be described as characteristic of the region and of the neighbouring Denmark (pl. 6, A and B): no fewer than thirty-four of them, from twenty-eight find-spots, have been found in the provinces of Gröningen, Friesland and, in a minor degree, Drenthe. It has indeed been suggested that their numbers are such as to indicate some sort of 'statuette cult' amongst the Frisian farmers, but if so the statuettes are too various to indicate its trend.

In addition to the statuettes, it has been calculated that the provinces mentioned have produced over fifty finds of *terra sigillata* and two hundred coins of the first-fourth centuries A.D., mostly from *terps*. The calculation is probably an underestimate. But it is scarcely necessary to emphasize that in the Frisian culture there was nothing which can be described as Roman in any significant sense. The Frisians, like the neighbouring Batavians to the south-west, had aided the Romans during the campaigns of Drusus and Germanicus, but revolted in A.D. 25 in consequence of tax-oppression and again in A.D. 69–70, when, once more with the Batavians, they achieved an enduring political independence. They appear, however, to have been an essentially peaceful folk, primarily stock-farmers (sheep and cattle, with some horses and pigs), but with an itch for the sea. They traded along the coast and perhaps via the canal whereby Drusus linked their territory with the Rhine in 12 B.C.; acting as carriers to and from the wealthy markets of Jutland and the Danish islands, and doubtless bartering their livestock. In the third century A.D., if not before, they were transporting cattle up the Rhine.[1]

Enough has been said to indicate broadly the environment in which Roman goods circulated, to a surprising extent, throughout a great part of Free Germany. Save in so far as Roman weapons and armour influenced the German war-gear (and *vice versa*), the impact of the one culture upon the other was, at any rate at first, of no great significance. The two societies were basically far too disparate for fruitful interaction, and Roman sherds or coins on the trampled floor of a German hut meant no more than did the Arretine dishes which strewed the squalid wigwams of Cunobelin at Colchester. But this contact at least served to show the resurgent German tribesmen of the Middle and Later Empire in what directions lay the rewards of victory, and must to that extent have stimulated and even oriented the earlier phases of their wanderings. The alluring taste for half-understood exotic things has often enough helped to bend the course of history.

(*d*) *Loot*. It cannot be doubted that in the turbulent times of the Later Empire the chronic pillaging of the Roman frontier-zone by Alamanni, Franks, and other German tribes or confederacies, to say nothing of free-lance piracy, contributed to the diffusion of Roman goods in Free Germany. In the next section the assemblage of Roman and romanizing material in the peat-bog hoards of Denmark

1. H. Wilkens in *Hansische Geschichtsblätter*, XIV (1908), 310.

will suggest sources of this kind. Rarely, however, can we expect discriminating evidence as between trade and plunder, and this heading need not therefore detain us long. Two examples will suffice. A bronze *situla* of the 'Hemmoor' type (p. 99) and probably of third-century date was recovered long ago from a barrow at Bjorska in the Vastmanland province of Sweden, some sixty miles N.W. of Stockholm. It had been used ultimately to hold the ashes of the dead, but it bears the inscription APOLLINI GRANNO DONVM AMMILLIVS CONSTANS PRAEF TEMPLI IPSIVS VSLLM ('Dedicated to Apollo Grannus by Ammillius Constans, warden of the temple') and, as temple property, is very unlikely to have been given or traded into native hands. The cult of Apollo Grannus had a special vogue in Raetia, and the distribution of the Hemmoor type is consistent with an origin in that quarter. The region was traversed by the Alamanni when they broke through the *limes* between the Danube and the Rhine in A.D. 213 and again in 260, and the *situla* doubtless found its way to its remote find-spot as loot on some occasion of the kind. Again, at a much earlier date, in wooded country somewhere between the Ems and the Weser had occurred one of the greatest disasters that ever befell the arms of Rome: the utter defeat and massacre of the three legions of Varus in A.D. 9 by the tribesmen of Arminius. This cataclysm marked the end of systematic Roman exploitation, political and commercial, towards the Elbe. But meanwhile the whole of the vast equipment of a considerable army passed into German hands; and, though we cannot hope to identify much of it at this long range, the remarkable concentration of Augustan gold around the scene of the catastrophe can scarcely be accidental.[1] It is a fair guess to recognize here some of the spilled treasury of Varus (fig. 6,

1. W. Knapke in *Acta Archaeologica*, XIV (Copenhagen, 1943), 58.

p. 75). On the other hand, the famous silver dinner service found buried at Hildesheim near Hanover at a considerable distance from the nearest Roman settlement may in fact be the campaigning outfit of a Roman commander, but cannot, as has been suggested, be ascribed to Varus or Germanicus, at any rate in its entirety, since, whatever the dates of its component parts, one of the pieces bears what is almost certainly an Antonine inscription.

(e) *Peat-bog or moss deposits.* Last but by no means least are the great assemblages of equipment which have been found during the past century in the mosses of Denmark. These mosses represent former meres or inlets of the sea which have in one way or another become isolated and so have degenerated first into marshland and then into peat-bog. Sealed successively by water and peat, objects often of a perishable kind have been preserved with a completeness rare in surface deposits, and the routine work of peat-cutters has combined with the vigilance of the Danish authorities to recover great quantities of this submerged material. Its presence in the former meres requires explanation, although any explanation must now in part be theoretical. Certain it is that in Scandinavia from the Stone Age onwards it was customary to dedicate objects of value – large flint axes, flint daggers and saws, bronze axes and swords, bronze trumpets, gold vessels, amber ornaments – by depositing them in the ground, in streams or springs, or in lakes. In the pre-Roman Iron Age this custom was continued and, it seems, given a new turn. Thus at Hjortspring in Danish Slesvig a thirty-foot boat was sunk some time in the fourth or third century B.C. with fragments of ringmail, fifty shields, eight swords, 170 spears with iron or bone points, and animal carcasses, and it is noteworthy that many of the weapons had been rendered intentionally unserviceable before their deposition. This procedure has recalled the statement of Orosius (v, 15) that, after their victory over the Romans at Orange in 105 B.C., the Cimbri

Fig. 6. Distribution of Augustan gold coinage resulting possibly from the Varus disaster, A.D. 9

and Teutons mutilated the captured gear, threw some of it into the river, drowned the horses and hanged the captives. 'All booty was destroyed in accordance with a new and

unaccustomed vow' – new and unaccustomed at any rate
to the historic world. Caesar (*B.G.* VI, 17) also refers to a
custom amongst the Gauls (a term which for him included
western Germans) of sacrificing 'such living things as they
have captured' and of gathering their other booty into
conspicuous heaps in hallowed spots. Similarly, at Toulouse,
as Strabo recounts (4. 1. 13), in 106 B.C. a Roman consul
pillaged a great treasure which had been 'stored away
partly in sacred enclosures, partly in sacred lakes' by its
Celtic owners. And on the Celtic fringe, a great mass of
Iron Age weapons and other gear found in a bog in
Anglesey in 1944 is best explained as the product of religious dedication. In one way and another, there is ample
precedent for a series of rich and famous peat-bog hoards
from Slesvig, Jutland, and Fyen dating from the troubled
third and fourth centuries A.D.

The contents of these peat-bogs need not be catalogued
here in great detail, but three of the discoveries may be
summarized to illustrate their range and character.[1] One
of the earliest of them (1858) was that of Thorsbjerg, so-
named from the adjacent 'Hill of Thor', a dozen miles
north-east of the town of Schleswig, now in Germany,
but until 1864 in Denmark. The site is that of a former
mere which may anciently have had an outlet to a neighbouring rivulet and so to the Firth of Sli three miles to the
south. The mere had become a mass of peat eleven feet
thick, and it was in a limited area within the lowest level
of this peat, and beneath it, that a remarkable collection
of objects was brought to light. A majority of them consisted of arms and armour, but ornaments, tools, agricultural implements, and even clothing were included.
Exceptional were parts of two Roman parade-helmets:

1. See C. Engelhardt, *Denmark in the Early Iron Age* (London,
1866).

one of thin bronze ornamented with wave- or fire-patterns, a wreathed star and possibly a thunderbolt, the other of silver lined with bronze and partially covered externally with thin gold plates. The latter helmet (pl. 8A) is composed of a face-piece (now lacking a vizor, if it ever had one) and a strapwork crown hinged to it, and is enriched with conventionalized hair and bands of small bosses on the crown and fringing the face. It would be a notable 'find' anywhere, but in this remote spot its interest is enhanced by the mystery of its immediate origin – scarcely an ordinary article of trade, but whether the product of a raid upon the Roman frontier or a diplomatic gift from the Roman world to some native chieftain can only be guessed. Certainly many other objects of Roman provenance were associated with it: fragmentary coats of mail; circular wooden shields,[1] either with round bronze bosses of Roman type – in one instance bearing the dotted name AEL. AELIANVS – or with conical bosses of native type, one with a Runic graffito; the bronze-fitted wooden scabbard of a Roman short-sword, and the wood or metal hilts and fittings of many other swords either of Roman manufacture or native adaptations; javelins (*pila* or angons); brooches, buckles, sandles and other gear. Two discs of gold- and silver-plated bronze incorporate or have been augmented by animals of a semi-Oriental type which the Goths spread across Europe from their far-off kingdom by the Black Sea. With all this was a great variety of more specifically native material, though with recurrent

1. It may be observed that on Roman monuments, mostly earlier than this hoard, Germans, like Celts, are shown ordinarily with oval or polygonal-oblong shields, and the Hjortspring hoard (above p. 74) includes oblong shields with rounded corners. Circular German-shields occur on the Column of Marcus Aurelius, however, and the round shield was characteristic of the Folk-wandering period. Cf. Tacitus, *Germ.* 43.

romanizing features: iron spears, spear-shafts of ash eight to ten feet long; long-bows of ash, about five feet long, and iron-shod arrows; whetstones, horse-harness, parts of wagon- or chariot-wheels, pottery; and five articles of woollen clothing, comprising two cloaks woven in a twill-pattern and in one case green with a yellow and black fringe, a shirt of which the long sleeves are ornamented with a diamond-pattern in the cloth, and two pairs of trousers with loops for the belt and 'feet' of a different and pat-terned cloth (pl. 10c). With the great hoard were thirty-seven Roman *denarii* ranging from Nero to Septimius Severus (A.D. 193-211) and sufficiently indicating the third century as a terminal date for the deposit.

About twenty miles north of Thorsbjerg, within three-quarters of a mile of the Als Sound of which it anciently formed an inlet, lies a narrow valley, now floored with peat, the famous moss of Nydam. Beneath the peat, at a depth of four to seven feet and covering an area of 10,000 square feet, was found in and after 1858 perhaps the most famous of the Danish bog-hoards.[1] Unfortunately, system-atic investigation was interrupted by the German invasion of 1864 and, in the words of the Danish investigator, 'the subsequent excavations at that spot, undertaken by German Princes and by a Prussian Baron, do not seem to have been carried on with the necessary care and intelligence'. Nevertheless, a wealth of material had already been recov-ered, representing much the same range as the Thorsbjerg hoard, but with additions and clearer detail.

The outstanding feature of the Nydam hoard was the presence of three boats, of which one, a clinker-built, sail-less yacht seventy-seven feet long, was removed almost intact. With the structure of these vessels we are not here concerned; it will suffice to note that they had been pierced

1. C. Engelhardt, *Nydam Mosefund* (Copenhagen, 1865).

and deliberately sunk, and that the objects found in and around them had apparently been on board them at the time of the sinking. These objects occurred in heaps tied together or wrapped in linen, and included 100 swords, some of them stamped with makers' names in Roman lettering (RICVS, RICCIM, COCILLVS, and others); between 500 and 600 heads of javelins and spears; 40 bows and 170 iron arrowheads; a scythe-blade and other tools; dress-fittings and ornaments; and 34 Roman *denarii*, extending from Vitellius to Macrinus (A.D. 217–18). The date of deposition was presumably, therefore, not distant from that of the Thorsbjerg hoard, though the character of certain of the Nydam objects suggests that they may be somewhat later, extending into the fourth century.

A third peat-bog hoard was recovered about the same time from the *Vimose* or Moss of Wi (i.e. temple), near the Firth of Odense in the north-east of the Danish island of Fyen.[1] Of 2,000 objects—swords, one with the stamp TASVIT, sheaths, spears, bows and arrows, a quiver, shields, and much other gear together with wooden bowls and pottery – some special mention may be made of two. One of these is a bronze ornament of Roman workmanship in the form of a griffin's head, probably from a helmet. The other is a complete shirt of mail, the only intact example from Free Germany of a type of armour abundantly represented in the bog-hoards by fragments. The shirt is of bronze-riveted iron rings about half an inch in diameter, has short sleeves, and is about three-and-a-half feet long, extending to above the knees (pl. 7B). Similar shirts of mail are familiar as worn by soldiery on the columns of Trajan and Marcus Aurelius and other Roman monuments, but the type is probably of Asiatic origin and was known to the Germans long before the Imperial period – witness the Hjortspring

1. C. Engelhardt, *Vimose Fundet* (Copenhagen, 1869).

hoard mentioned above. With the Vimose hoard were coins of Marcus Aurelius and Faustina the Younger, implying a date after A.D. 180, but insufficient for precision.

A review of these hoards and of others like them indicates certain common and significant features. First, they are mostly within easy reach of the sea, and are characteristic of the wealthiest region of Free Germany – namely, the eastern side of the Jutland peninsula, and the Danish islands. Outside this region the only find at all comparable is a later and much simpler one from Kvalsund in Norway. Secondly, each hoard certainly or probably represents a single deposit rather than a gradual or casual accumulation. Witness the bundled cargoes of Nydam, with shields in one part, arrows and wooden vessels in another, a group of swords in yet another; or the fact that at Thorsbjerg specific classes of objects were likewise found in separate heaps – for example, several layers of shields pinned together by a javelin which had been thrust through them, or a concentration of gold objects, or of mail, in which spear-heads and small arms might be collected and wrapped. Thirdly, most of the objects had been deliberately damaged, often not in a fashion which can be ascribed to the incidents of battle. The shield-bosses are bent and crumpled and broken, a wooden sheath from Thorsbjerg is cut in two and the pieces placed one on the other, many sheaths are deprived of some or all of their mountings, mail shirts are cut and rolled up and the pieces sometimes placed carefully in clay pots, lances are fantastically twisted. At least one of the Nydam boats had been intentionally and drastically destroyed, and the two boats at Kvalsund had been deliberately shattered so that no two timbers were left fastened together. More than that, though human skeletons are almost certainly absent from the bog-finds, the bones of slaughtered animals, particularly horses, are abundant, and the butchering has been carried out with an astonishing thoroughness. Thus a horse's skull from Nydam bears no fewer than ten sword-cuts, and others show similar treatment. At the Vimose many horses' skulls and bones were found splintered and hewn to pieces beside chopping-blocks which had been extensively used. Another horse at Nydam had an iron arrowhead in the left shoulder and a second in the ribs. Detached heads of horses at the same place still had their bits in their mouths. Equipment and animals alike had been mutilated systematically before being consigned to the mere or inlet in which the peat had subsequently covered and preserved them.

Two other observations may be added. The hoards, in so far as they are datable, belong to the period of the Later Empire, the third or fourth century A.D. And they are linked predominantly with the Roman world. Many of their contents were made within the boundaries of the Empire; many others betray the native craftsman with a knowledge of Roman things; and, if from time to time a semi-Oriental element, such as a Scythian-looking animal pattern or perhaps the bows, may have been derived from south-eastern Europe, we have to remember that by this time a 'Gothic' zone extended from the Baltic to the Black Sea and that from this zone tribal groups – Burgundians, Alamanni, and others – were pushing westwards and familiarizing the West with south Russian modes.

If now all these various facts are added up, they make a not unimpressive total. At a number of points readily accessible to a society based largely upon the sea, great assemblages of war-gear were sacrificed in a traditional manner, by slighting and submersion. The picture is, as we have seen, exactly that painted by Orosius speaking of the Cimbri and Teutons at Orange, or by Caesar speaking of the Gauls in general. Whoever the rulers of the Cimbric

peninsula were in the third century A.D., they or their
tributary tribesmen were bringing in to their religious
centres great quantities of loot, mostly obtained either by
piracy in the Baltic or in the English Channel, where the
British and Gaulish shores were now specifically fortified
against Saxon sea-raiders, or, perhaps more probably, from
battlefields somewhere within reasonable range of the
Roman frontier. In the absence of precise dates for the
hoards, a closer context is not feasible. Suffice it to recall
that in A.D. 213 the confederation of German tribes known
as the Alamanni burst through the Raetian frontier and
heralded a long age of increasing German pressure on the
West. In A.D. 257–8 another confederation, the Franks,
from between the Ems and the Rhine, swept through Gaul
and into Spain. Two years later the Alamanni were again
on the move; they carried destruction across the *limes*
into Gaul and, though they were turned by Postumus as
'Emperor of the Gauls', the old frontier territory east of
the upper Rhine was never again reoccupied by the Romans
in force. Here are a few of many occasions when in the
third century Free Germans could have brought home
great quantities of frontier loot to their gods in their
northern meres, just as in earlier times the Romans had
brought German booty home to their Capitol. It may be
added that there is some archaeological evidence for the
abrupt extension of the native culture of the Danish islands
to the Jutland peninsula about A.D. 200 (above, p. 46). But
it is no more compulsory to postulate that the bog-finds of
Denmark represent great battles fought in Slesvig or on
Fyen than that the Roman triumphs of a Germanicus or
a Domitian imply victories in the Forum Romanum.
Whatever their precise and immediate origin, the general
significance of the peat-bog hoards is plain enough as a
picturesque footnote to third and fourth-century history.

CHAPTER FIVE

FREE GERMANY: THE IMPORTS

IN this section selected groups of Roman imports into Free Germany are discussed summarily in respect of date and distribution. No attempt is made to cover the whole field; the maps and lists prepared by Dr H. J. Eggers in 1951[1] have made any such attempt unnecessary for some time to come. But samples of the coin-finds, metal-wares, and glass will serve to illustrate and amplify some of the data collected in the previous sections, and will demonstrate the richness of the field. We begin with a general indication of the evidence of the coins.

COINS[2]

Between the Rhine frontier and Latvia, between the Danube and Gotland, some thousands of Roman coins – gold, silver, and 'copper' – found their way into the soil of Free Germany and Scandinavia from the time of Augustus onwards. The circumstances of their finding and the significance of their distribution have been discussed by a number of scholars, notably by S. Bolin, whose conclusions hold the field.[3] His detailed analyses are not here recounted, but some of the more general aspects are necessary to our picture, and are in fact implicit in certain of the previous sections.

The coins occur singly and in hoards; of the latter more than 400 are known, and not a few of the single coins may in fact represent ill-recorded hoards. They are found in

1. See Bibliography, p. 215. 2. Pl. 11 B and fig. 7.
3. *Fyndan av romerska mynt i det fria Germanien* (Lund, 1926); résumé in *Bericht des Deutsches Arch. Inst.* 1929 (Frankfort, 1930), 86ff.

graves, on settlement-sites, in peat-bogs, and at unrelated find-spots. The extent nevertheless to which they circulated as actual currency amongst the tribesmen was doubtless relatively slight. When we come to consider the Roman coinage of India, the probability will emerge that there the imported gold and silver coins were used largely in bulk, as bullion guaranteed in quality and perhaps weight by the imperial stamp, but rarely distributed as currency: a supposition reinforced by the absence there of Roman 'copper' coins before the fourth century, and by the deliberate mutilation of Roman gold. The likelihood of a similar attitude in inner Germany is supported by the statement of Tacitus (*Germ.* 5) that 'the Germans nearest to us value gold and silver for their use in trade . . . The peoples of the interior employ barter.' Consistently with this, in the time of Tacitus, at the end of the first century A.D., copper coinage was rare in Germany.[1]　Later, on the other hand, presumably as a result of commercial experience, this coinage flowed more freely, and before the end of the Antonine period (second century) was not infrequently included in graves as far afield as East Prussia. After this time, copper must have been used fairly widely as 'small change' in the normal processes of monetary circulation, doubtless encouraged by the fact that, with the deterioration of the silver after Trajan and particularly after Septimius Severus, there was an increasing approximation in metal-value between the two categories.

That the quality of the Roman silver was carefully watched by the German traders is clear from the further statement of Tacitus that the Germans preferred 'money that is old and familiar, *denarii* with the notched edge

1. Only thirty-six stray copper coins are recorded from West Germany and Holland (outside the Roman frontier) of dates prior to the end of the first century A.D.

and the type of the two-horse chariot' (pl. 11 B). The barbarian habit of adhering to certain well-known types of
foreign coinage is familiar enough, an example being the
retention of Maria Theresa dollars in modern Abyssinia.
Even the Athenians of the fifth-century B.C. found it
politic to retain their archaic coin-dies, and Celtic moneyers
of the first centuries B.C.–A.D. adhered largely to a Macedonian type of the fourth century B.C. But the conserva-
tism of Tacitus's Germans was not unreasoned; for in
A.D. 63 Nero had reduced the silver-content of the *denarius*
and so enhanced the popularity of previous issues in remote
markets where intrinsic worth rather than state guarantee
was the basis of confidence. Later a similar ponding-back of
pre-Severan *denarii* seems to have occurred in the third
century after the further devaluation of the currency by
Septimius Severus. It may be doubted, however, whether
the imported coinage ever entered significantly, even as
bullion, into the domestic trade of Free Germany; rather
may we suspect that its primary use to the German was as
a medium for the purchase of other imports from Roman
or sub-Roman merchants, of whose penetration into unconquered territories there are many examples. In favour
of this supposition is the scarcity of pre-Neronic silver in
German hoards later than A.D. 107 when Trajan finally
called it in. Most of it must already – or soon afterwards –
have found its way back across the Roman frontier.[1]

In summary, then, it is to be supposed that in the peripheral trade of Free Germany, where contact with traders
from the Roman world was recurrent, Roman coins circulated in so far as their metal-value was intrinsically acceptable; in the interior and the outlands they were used
variously in bulk as bullion, or individually as curiosities,
gifts, ornaments, and sometimes as funerary equipment;

1. Or, as pure silver, into the melting-pot.

rarely as a local instrument of exchange, since the Germans, unlike the Celts, were unfamiliar with a monetary system and cannot readily or widely have adopted this alien usage.

Roman gold coinage was unpopular in Germany prior to the fourth century. Its value was presumably too high for normal use. Tacitus (*Germ.* 5) observes that the Germans of the interior tried to get silver in preference to gold; only those 'nearest us' valued both gold and silver. The archaeological evidence confirms the statement. Reference has been made (p. 73) to the scatter of Augustan gold within range of the Varus disaster of A.D. 9. Apart from this, a small hoard of six *aurei* of Tiberius, Claudius, and Nero, has been found at Tensfelderau, Kr. Segeberg, in Schleswig-Holstein; and another of Tiberius is recorded from West Germany. This modest total may be compared with upwards of thirteen first-century hoards of *denarii* in the same region. A hoard of *aurei* of the same date from Bohemia fits in with the historical relationship between the Marcomanni and the empire at this period. Other stray finds of *aurei* from West Germany and Holland of dates prior to A.D. 100 all lie sufficiently near the frontier to require no other explanation.

To the second century A.D. no gold hoards are ascribed, although occasional gold coins of that century, usually pierced or otherwise adapted for ornament, penetrated to Thuringia and Bavaria. Gold of the third century in Germany or Denmark was deposited mostly in the fourth century, when Constantinian *solidi* took the field and were continued by an increasing succession of gold deposits into the fifth century, particularly in Eastern Germany. There the fluid tribal situation – particularly the Gothic and Hunnish migrations – had set up a new current of intercourse between the Baltic and the Black Sea, and new if superficial standards of luxury were emerging under the influence of forceful contact with the Byzantine world.

The distributions of Roman coinage in Free Germany have already constituted a major basis for the section dealing with routes and markets (p. 26) and, save by maps (figs. 2, p. 27, and 7), need not be amplified in detail for the general picture which is the purpose of this book. It will suffice

Fig. 7. Distribution of Roman coins in Free Germany
prior to A.D. 250

to add that under the steadying influence of firm Imperial rule hoards, the non-recovery of which is a sure symptom of a time of trouble, are of rare occurrence in the earlier half of the second century; they do not again become emphatic until the long period of disturbance which began with the Marcomannic war of Marcus Aurelius in A.D. 167. That war was itself merely a focus of unrest extending far beyond the limits of Bohemia. For example, of hoards ending with coins of Marcus Aurelius, five are known from western Germany, three from the mouth of the Vistula, others from Posen, Schleswig-Holstein, and Sweden. The Vistula hoards, added to those of Commodus from the same region, may represent a reaction to the earlier movements of the Goths from their Swedish homeland on their long march towards south-eastern Europe (p. 43). But the equation of particular coin-groups with inchoate historical phases of this kind is liable to be an arbitrary business and cannot be stressed. So again a further suggestion, that a series of third-century silver hoards and gold coins, extending down to the emperor Probus (A.D. 276–82), marks the migration of Burgundians and Vandals from east-central Europe towards Gaul about A.D. 278, is of questionable value. It is in fact possible to isolate a number of these finds in an appropriate belt across Germany through southern Brandenburg, Saxony and Thuringia, but only by applying the blind eye to wide variations in dating and distribution. Certainly without the historical background no comparable movement could fairly have been deduced from the coin-evidence as it stands. On the whole, in so confused and turbulent a territory as Free Germany it is best to restrict the use of coins primarily to the analysis of main routes and concentrations, as an amplification of other archaeological evidence, and above all as a chronological control.

VESSELS OF SILVER AND GOLD

Free Germany has yielded an impressive quantity of Roman silver-ware, the combined product doubtless of commerce, warfare, and diplomacy. Pride of place must be given to the great hoard discovered in 1868 at Hildesheim, south of Hanover, where it had been carefully hidden in a pit about four feet by three feet dug to a depth of some five feet below the former level. Including fragments, it comprised about seventy pieces, and is one of the more remarkable collections of silver known from the ancient world (pls. 7C, 9, A and B). Most of the pieces must have been made within the century 50 B.C. – A.D. 50 with a bias towards the early Augustan period, but the name, Marcus Aurelius, stippled on the base of one of them suggests, without absolute proof, that they were not buried before the name came into prominence in the second century A.D. In the circumstances, guesses as to the conditions of burial are unprofitable. No relevant military or civil site has been identified in the vicinity.

Amongst the contents of the hoard[1] were half a dozen dishes, eight plates and trays, eight bowls, nine cups, two urns, a bucket, four *paterae*, two tripod-tables and a candelabrum, all of silver, sometimes partially gilt: but whether the total represented the luxury equipment of a general officer's 'mess' or whether it was otherwise assembled cannot be deduced with any approach to certainty. It is not merely in quantity that the hoard is outstanding, for two at least of the pieces are unsurpassed amongst the surviving examples of the Graeco-Roman silversmith's craft. One of these is a two-handled dish, elaborately ornamented with honeysuckle and lotus patterns and with a seated figure of Athena set as a central *emblema* in high relief (pl. 9B). Except for the arms, face, and neck, the figure is (or was) gilded, and certain elements in the floral design are also picked out with gilding. The quality of the modelling, particularly in the studied but not unrealistic grace of the drapery, reflects the living tradition of Hellenistic sculpture and gives the figure an independent value as a work of art. Where it was made is disputable: Asia Minor and Alex-

1. E. Pernice and F. Winter, *Der Hildesheimer Silberfund* (Berlin, 1901).

andria are two obvious competitors: but the artist was certainly a Greek.

The other outstanding vessel is a dish with a central relief or *emblema* representing the infant Hercules grasping two snakes, framed by a tendril-pattern issuing from the tails of two griffins and interspersed with birds (pl. 9A). The pattern, the child's clothing, and the snakes were gilded. There is evidence that the *emblema* is an insertion, and the contrast of its skilled workmanship with the relative coarseness of the tendril adds proof that the two parts did not originally belong to the same vessel. The naturalistic child's head, rendered in the round, is a good example of late Hellenistic genre, in contrast with the more academic Athena of the dish described above.

Other pieces in this famous collection must here be passed by with scarcely a mention: the dishes with *emblemata* representing Attis and Cybele, bowls with the elaborate, naturalistic floral patterns which delighted the Augustan taste, urns with satyrs' masks, herms, and theatrical grotesques. Three or four of the pieces show a coarser, less academic handling which has suggested the possibility of a provincial origin for them. Such are an oblong tray (pl. 7C), with vigorous representations of duck rising from the water or diving below it, and, above all, two conical cups with bold if somewhat uncouth friezes of animals, rosettes, and leaf-patterns. These may date from a time nearer that of the burial of the hoard, and may be additions to it from a Gaulish source. Unhappily, surviving examples of Gaulish craftsmanship of the kind are too rare to offer satisfactory proof of this attribution.

If we turn from the Hildesheim hoard to other finds of silverware, we are at once on familiar ground; for of eleven sites which have produced such ware, no fewer than nine are those of 'chieftains' graves' of the Lübsow group. The

scyphi of Hoby on the island of Laaland, of Dollerup in
Jutland, and of Lübsow I in Pomerania have already been
described (p. 53ff.), and, with the exception of a minor
cup from Hoby, attributed to a Mediterranean (Graeco-
Roman) origin. Others may be ascribed rather to provincial
workshops. A pair of plain but graceful cups from a grave
at Byrsted in Jutland has been regarded, without certainty
or perhaps probability, as Gaulish; but it is likely enough
that small silver bowls of late Roman date, vaguely imitating cut-glass vessels, on the one hand from Haagerup in
Fyen, Nordrup in Zealand, and Leuna in Saxony, and on
the other hand from Chaoucre, Dep. Aisne, were made in
Gaul (pl. 8B). A provincial origin has been proposed for
the silver cups from Dollerup in Jutland (p. 59); and
others from Mollerup, also in Jutland, from the second
grave at Lübsow in Pomerania, from Leg Piekarski in
Poland, and from Holubic near Prague[1] all show un-Roman
features, but have not been satisfactorily identified with
specific provincial schools. Their normally excellent
manufacture, the recurrent use of gilding to emphasize
the pattern, and their generally classical types may be taken
to indicate origins within the Empire. There is at present
no clear hint of any production of this kind and quality
within Free Germany itself. It may be added that, with the
exception of the bowls from Haagerup, most of the silver
vessels from Free Germany belong by type and association
to the first two centuries of the Empire, with emphasis on
the first century rather than the second. In other words,
they largely precede the full development of Romano-
Gallic craftsmanship.

The region of the Black Sea remains at present an
unknown quantity in the luxury trade beyond the fron-

1. For these cups, see especially O. Voss in *Acta Arch.* XIX (1948),
252ff.

tiers. It may be conjectured that from or through this
region came to Varpelev in Zealand an elaborate cup of
blue glass with frame and pierced foliage-overlay of silver,
incorporating the Greek greeting Ευτυχως (pl. 5B). With
the cup was a coin of Probus (A.D. 276–82), and
the burial may not in fact be earlier than the fourth
century, but we may recall that from the latter part of the
third century south Russia was linked by a more or less
continuous Gothic zone with central Europe and the
Baltic (p. 43).[1] A similar south-eastern origin has been
ascribed to the silver goblets from a well-known find at
Valløby in Zealand. The decoration of these goblets, in
particular a frieze of backward-looking animals below the
rim, is consistent with a South Russian origin, and the
Goths may again be suspected as the carriers. Against this
supposition is the fact that amongst the associated objects
was a *sigillata* bowl signed by the potter Comitialis, who
worked at Rheinzabern in western Germany during the
latter half of the second century, and this date, if accepted
literally, is earlier than that of the Gothic kingdom by the
Black Sea. Transit up the Danube valley and thence northwards along one or other of the well-trodden trade-routes
from Carnuntum is an alternative possibility which would
reconcile date and probable origin without involving the
Goths; and a similar path, at any rate from Carnuntum
onwards, may have been taken by an attractive silver cup,
of low cylindrical form with relief ornament representing
masks and a griffin bringing down a stag, found at Ostropataka in Czechoslovakia. This cup is, however, of late

1. A second-century date and an Italian origin have been ascribed
to this cup, and the occurrence of an heirloom in a late grave is not
impossible. But I see no reason why the cup should not be of the
third century, and the Eastern Mediterranean is a more probable
source than Italy.

date and may equally well have passed through Gothic hands beyond the frontier.

The only recorded gold vessel of classical type is a plain chalice about six-and-a-half inches high, found at Ostropataka with the silver cup just mentioned, and presumably of similar origin and date. The two famous golden drinking-horns from Gallehus in Sleswig,[1] though possibly of late Roman date, have nothing to do with Roman craftsmanship or usage.

BRONZE WARE

Of bronze vessels, more than 850 have been found in Free Germany (with Scandinavia), about half of them in Jutland and the Baltic islands. The total is impressive, particularly when it be recalled that sites other than graves have scarcely contributed to it. Apart from the fact that relatively few settlements of the period have been explored, the chance of survival of a metal vessel on an occupation-site is very much less than in a grave. At the same time, it is not to be assumed that the custom of burying these vessels with the dead was coextensive with their total distribution. An examination of the burials in the vicinity of the gulf of Danzig has already demonstrated the contrary (p. 40).

Selected examples must here suffice to illustrate this great mass of material. The series begins, so far as we are concerned, with a number of imports dating from the end of the first century B.C. and the first decade of the first century A.D., and may here be represented by two distinctive types: a *situla* or wine-bucket with a pair of confronted dolphins at the base of the handle-strap, and a saucepan or casserole with a swan's head on each side of

1. Conveniently accessible in H. Shetelig and H. Falk, *Scandinavian Archaeology* (Oxford, 1937), p. 208 and pl. 36.

Fig. 8. Distribution of early types of Roman bronze vessels

the pierced end of the handle (fig. 8). Of the former, six or seven examples of this period are recorded: four or five from Bohemia and the Thuringian border, one from the Oder valley in Brandenburg, one from Mecklenburg near the Elbe, and one from Hoby in Zealand – all with a single exception from cremation-burials. Predecessors of the same general type had found their way in the first century B.C. into the river-valleys of the North German plain as far eastwards as the Vistula and the Passarge, and one had even ventured as far north as Sweden. Their ultimate origin was doubtless in Italy, where Capua dominates the archaeological scene, but whether at this early date they travelled northwards from the Danube or found their way more circuitously through the Celtic lands is not at present clear. The pattern becomes unmistakable, however, in the first decade A.D. The concentration of late Augustan types in Bohemia reflects the regime of the romanizing Marcomannian king Maroboduus and the recorded activity of Roman traders amongst his tribesmen (p. 23). The old Aquileia-Danube route was now systematized via Carnuntum in the methodical Augustan manner, and a reasonably regular traffic along it was the natural sequel. Dolphin-buckets and swan-saucepans travelled that way, and no fewer than twenty of the latter have been recovered from Marcomannian graves, with an outlier near the valley of the lower March as a pointer. Further north, the swan-saucepans reached the valleys of the Oder and the Weser, but only one of them made Scandinavia – a strangely isolated example from a grave at Kvåle, far up the Sogne fiord eighty miles north-east of Bergen. Only two of them approached the Baltic coast, and there is no reason for associating the distribution of either type specifically within the amber trade.

Other early Imperial types confirm these distributions: for example, buckets or *situlae* with a human mask on the attachments of the handle-loops such as that already described from Lübsow (p. 62), *paterae* with ram's-head handles, and round-bottomed ladles or strainers with oarshaped handles, the bowls of the strainers pierced at first in the form of a maeander. These imports extend the map-pattern slightly towards Poland and Sweden, but the main bulk of them remains concentrated in central Europe and Denmark. Italy – in particular, Campania – was still the source of supply, and the Carnuntum route remained the principal approach. As the first century wore on, however, a variation began to emerge: after the flight of Maroboduus in A.D. 18 (p. 37), Bohemia, home of the Marcomanni, gradually lost the commercial impetus which the king had given to it, and was increasingly by-passed by the Italian trade with the north. An illustration will make this clear. Partially contemporary with the swan-handled saucepans already mentioned, but outlasting them, were other types marked by a swan-less half-round or circular piercing through the handle. These scarcely occur in Bohemia, but are abundant further north, particularly in the Danish islands. Eggers notes that, of those with the circular piercing, only two have been recorded from Bohemia as against no fewer than fifty-one from Denmark, mostly from inhumation-graves (fig. 9, p. 97). The map-pattern, now focused on *c.* A.D. 50 and later, still suggests a Danubian rather than a Gaulish or North Sea approach, but against this must be set the cessation of the productive graves towards the west. In the circumstances, it is, as often, impossible, in the interpretation of the map, to estimate the extent to which the distribution of a burial custom may distort the archaeological distribution. One other early type calls for remark even in a summary list. This is a plain convex-sided bronze pail about nine inches high, with simple eyelet for the handle, known as the 'Eastland' type. Ten of these occur in the territory of the Marcomanni, whom they presumably reached in the first quarter of the first century A.D. For the rest, they cover what we may now

Bronze statuette of Harpocrates from Taxila, Punjab. Nearly
¼ (See p. 189)

1

(A) Silver cup from a 'chieftain's' grave at Hoby, Laaland. ⅛ (See p. 54)

(B) Silver cup, partially gilt, from a 'chieftain's' grave at Dollerup, Denmark. ½ (See p. 58)

Roman bronze vessels and glass with drinking horns, etc., in a 'chieftain's' grave at Juellinge, Laaland. (Two portions of the same grave.)

Roman vessels of bronze (*1* and *4*) and glass (*2* and *3*) from 'chieftain's' graves at Juellinge, Laaland. *1* and *4*, ¼; *2* and *3* ⅓ (See p. 60)

(A) Silver cup, partially gilt from the 'chieftain's' grave, Lubsow I. ⅛ (See p. 62)

(B) Glass cup with silver overlay from Varpelev, Zealand. ½ (See p. 92)

(A) Bronze statuette of Mars, from Tybjerggaard, Denmark. ⅓ (See p. 71)

(B) Bronze statuette of Jupiter, from Ezinge, Holland. ⅔ (See p. 71)

6

(A) Bronze jug from a 'chieftain's' grave at Hoby, Laaland. ½ (See p. 55)

(B) Shirt of Mail from the Vimose, Fyen. ⅟₁₆ (See p. 79)

(C) Silver tray from the Hildesheim hoard, Hanover. ⅓ (See pp. 89, 90)

(A) Silver parade-helmet from the moss of Thorsbjerg, Denmark. $\frac{1}{6}$ (See p. 77)

(B) Silver bowl imitating glasswork from Haagerup, Fyen. $\frac{1}{2}$ (See p. 91)

(A) Silver dish from the Hildesheim hoard. ¼ (See pp. 89, 90)

(B) Silver dish from the Hildesheim hoard. ¼ (See p. 89)

9

(A) Glass beaker, probably of south Russian origin, from Nordrup, Zealand. $\frac{2}{5}$ (See p. 107)

(B) Amphora from a burial in the Fezzan. About $\frac{1}{12}$ (See p. 123)

(C) Woollen trousers from the moss of Thorsbjerg, Denmark. $\frac{1}{20}$ (See p. 78)

(A) Roman lamp from the 'palace' of Tin Hinan, in the Hoggar. ¾ (See p. 136)

(B) Early Roman silver coins from Denmark. ⅓ (See p. 85)

(A) Painted glass cup of 'Nordrup-Jesendorf' type, from Himlingoje, Denmark. ⅔ (See p. 106)

(B) Cup of green glass with 'claw' decoration, from Vedsted, Zealand. ½ (See p. 107)

(A) Green glass beakers from Orslev, Underskov, Zealand (left) and Killerup, Fyen (right). ¼ (See p. 108)

(B) Green glass drinking-horn from Laerkenfeldt, Denmark. ¼ (See p. 108)

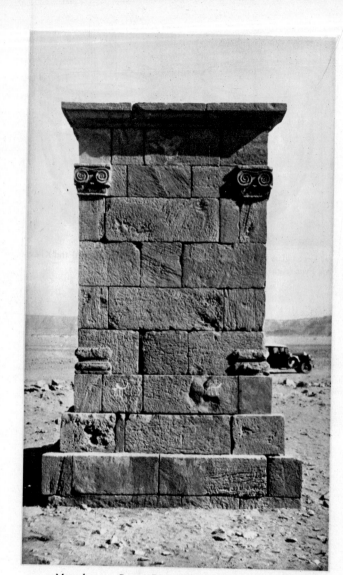

Mausoleum at Germa, Fezzan. Height 15 feet. (See p. 126)

Indian ivory statuette from Pompeii. $\frac{3}{5}$ (See p. 163)

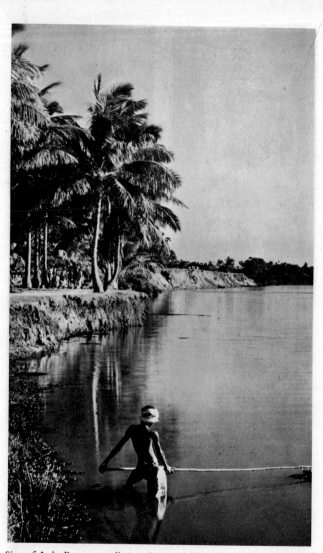

Site of Indo-Roman trading-station at Arikamedu, near Pondicherry, South India. (See p. 173)

(A) Arikamedu: brick foundations projecting from river-bank. (See p. 173)

(B) Arikamedu: excavations in progress, 1945. (See p. 173)

Roman and Indian coins from a hoard found at Eyyal, near Trichur, in Cochin State, South India. ¾ (See pp. 166, 169) Silver: Indian (3 coins) and denarii of Augustus (4 coins). Gold: Aurei of Tiberius and Trajan (top row), Claudius (centre) and Nero (bottom row). ¾

18

(A) Arikamedu: *1-6*, fragments of Arretine dishes (1 stamped VIBIE) : 7, Roman lamp. ⅓ (See pp. 173, 177)

(B) Arikamedu: fragments of Roman amphorae. ⅔ (See pp. 173, 177)

19

Bronze statuette of Poseidon, from Kolhapur, Western India. Nearly ¼
(See p. 180)

(B) Cameo from Karvan, Baroda, Western India. Nearly ½ (See p. 181)

(A) Handle of bronze jug from Akota, Baroda, Western India. ¾ (See p. 181)

(C) Handle of bronze jug from Akota, Baroda, Western India. ½ (See p. 181)

Terracotta imitations of coins of Tiberius (obverses), from Kondapur,
Hyderabad State. ¼ (See p. 181)

Reverses of coins in plate 22. ⅓ (See p. 181)

(A) Bronze jug from Kolhapur, Western India. ⅜ (See p. 180)

(B) Silver repoussé *emblema* representing Dionysus, from Taxila, Punjab. ¾ (See p. 189)

Air-view of part of Taxila (Sirkap), Punjab, as excavated. (See p. 187)

Stone frieze from Taxila, Punjab. Length 15 in. (See p. 191)

Stone relief showing Laocoön and the Trojan Horse, from the North-West Frontier Province. ⅙ (See p. 191)

(A) Stucco head of a satyr, from Taxila. $\frac{3}{8}$ (See p. 190)

(B) Stucco head of an infant, from Taxila. $\frac{1}{2}$ (See p. 190)

(A) Terracotta head base on the Apollo Belvedere, from Charsada, North-West Frontier Province. ⅓ (See p. 191)

(B) Stucco head of a youth, from Taxila. ¼ (See p. 190)

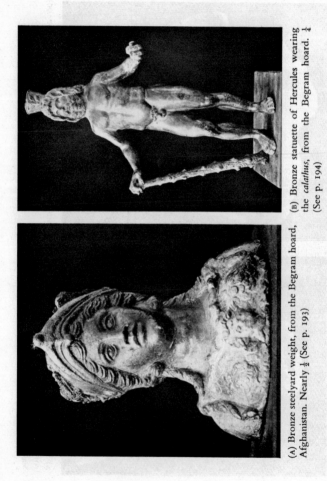

(A) Bronze steelyard weight, from the Begram hoard, Afghanistan. Nearly ½ (See p. 193)

(B) Bronze statuette of Hercules wearing the *calathus*, from the Begram hoard. ¼ (See p. 194)

(B) Bronze figurine of armed horseman, from the Begram hoard. ⅔ (See p. 194)

(A) Roman glass beaker with painted decoration, from the Begram hoard. ½ (See p. 194)

31

Stucco *emblemata* representing the grape-harvest (*below*) and
Athena (*above*), from the Begram hoard. $\frac{1}{2}$ (See p. 195)

term the conventional early first-century zone in central
Europe and Denmark; but the type lasted on well into the
second century and perhaps even later (p. 60) and, unlike
the contemporary types already discussed, spread across

Fig. 9. Distribution of Roman *paterae* with circular-piercing

D

into Norway and Sweden, where, excluding the Swedish
islands, over fifty examples have been found (fig. 10). In
Norway they are probably all derived from cremation-
graves, in which they conveniently contained the ashes.

Fig. 10. Distribution of 'the poor-man's bucket'

In Sweden they occasionally occur also as grave-furniture with inhumations. Why this unusual spread into the far north?

The reason which has been given by more than one writer is doubtless the correct one: these vessels are the simplest and cheapest of their kind, and were alone within the purchasing power of the poorer folk of the hills and fiords beyond the Baltic; only the relatively wealthy aristocracy of Denmark and the German Plain could afford elaborate and costly bronzes such as those of many of the chieftains' graves. The differential factor here, therefore, was an economic or sociological one, and had little or nothing to do with burial custom or trade facilities. The archaeological lesson is worth nothing.

By the Later Empire – the third and fourth centuries – changes had taken place in the orientation of the traffic in bronze vessels, as of other commodities, though in bulk the trade showed little change. Save for the occurrence of two types of bucket or *situla* (Eggers, maps 17 and 20), Bohemia was commercially no longer on the map. Again with these questionable exceptions, trade with Italy had been replaced by a considerable trade with Gaul and an intermittent trade with the Black Sea region. Denmark, and in particular Zealand, still remained a major customer, but now Thuringia and the lowlands between the Elbe and the lower Rhine were substantial rivals, whilst Poland is occasionally represented and would doubtless make a more impressive showing if more adequately explored.

To illustrate these new trends, no better example can be taken than the so-called 'Hemmoor' buckets (fig. 11, p. 100). These are simple handled bowls seven to nine inches high on a footstand, with a linear or, occasionally, figured zone below the rim. They occur along and behind the Rhine-Neckar-Danube frontier, not infrequently in hoards, which

have been associated with the break-through of the Alamanni in these parts about A.D. 258. Their Gaulish or West
German origin is certain, and their manufacture has been
variously ascribed to Cologne and to the neighbourhood

Fig. 11. Distribution of 'Hemmoor' buckets

of Aachen; an inscribed example from as far afield as Sweden may have come from Raetia (p. 73). An analysis of their distribution beyond the frontier suggests interesting interpretations. In Denmark and Mecklenburg they are found largely with inhumation-burials, and the same rule applies to Thuringia; in Lausitz they are associated with, but do not contain, cremations, and are often 'ritually broken' in accordance with a widespread funeral custom. From the mouth of the Elbe to the lower Rhine they occur also in cremation-graves, but here as containers of the burnt bones. How far these variations may be equated with tribal groups is a dangerous speculation which must await some future analysis of the associated native cultures. In any event, the task is complicated almost beyond hope by the fluid condition of the German tribes in the third century; and to suggest, as has been done, that the Lausitz folk were Burgundians and the western group Saxons is to outpace both the historical and the archaeological evidence.

These vessels, and others of the same phase – straight-sided bronze basins, late bronze strainers with oar-shaped handle and flat base (Eggers types 78–88 and 161), were doubtless distributed by the standard routes: the tributary valleys of the Rhine as far south as the Main, and the North Sea coast extended by a land-traverse across the base of the Jutland peninsula. It is worthy of note that five examples reached the southern coast of Norway.

Mention of Norway may remind us that, except for the islands, Norway and Sweden have mostly been peripheral to our study. Now, however, in the fourth century, on one occasion they dominate the scene. A group of bucket-handled bronze vessels with cylindrical neck and sharply rounded or carinated body (Eggers types 11–14, 'Westland type') occurs in nineteen cremation-burials in Norway and Sweden, reaching as far north as the Trondheim fiord on the west and Sundsvall on the east; the latter point may have been reached by a land-route across country from the former (fig. 12). This remarkable distribution is emphasized by the fact that only four examples are known from Free

Fig. 12. Distribution of bronze vessels of Westland type

Germany south of the Baltic – one each from inhumation-burials on Fyen and in Mecklenburg, one from a cremation at the mouth of the Elbe, and one from a peat deposit by the middle reaches of the river. Owing to the general absence of associated goods from the northern graves, the chronology of these vessels is largely theoretical, though the late Roman dating is fairly well established by the two inhumation-burials. They are later, perhaps considerably later, than the 'Hemmoor' type, and may well, as Eggers suggests, spill over into the fifth century. A similar suspicion arises in regard to other late groups of bronze or glass with a comparable though less isolated distribution (p. 47). If so, they are a not undramatic expression of coastal concentration and activity on the eve of the great Folk-wandering. But the evidence is at present of a sketchy character.

Traffic with southern or south-eastern Europe, in particular the Black Sea region, has already been illustrated tentatively (p. 42) by reference to certain types of fluted bronze vessel which, rather by process of elimination than by direct evidence, have been ascribed alternatively to that source or to Italy (fig. 13, p. 104). Of the two main types of fluted bowl, the earlier, which seems to emerge a little before A.D. 200, has a rounded profile, fine fluting, and a twisted handle with attachment-loops flanked by swans' heads. The type-site is Gile, near Oslo, and the type is, curiously enough, relatively common in Norway, though it also occurs on eight sites in East Prussia and Pomerania. The later variety has upright sides, coarser fluting, and a plain handle, and is known as the Valløby type from a site in Zealand. This also appears in the lands beside the lower Vistula. Along the Gaulish frontier the general type occurs rarely and only in circumstances which can be explained by garrison-movement from central or eastern Europe. In Italy the type is not known, but our knowledge there of post-Pompeiian metalwork is slight. It may occur on the margins of the Black Sea, but these are at present barred to research. The most certain and significant feature attending it is its presence in some force in East Prussia, northern

Fig. 13. Distribution of fluted bronze bowls

Poland, and eastern Pomerania, a region approached from
the south-east by the river-arteries of the Vistula and the
Dniester; and Italy is perhaps less likely as the starting-
point than are the obscured markets and factories of south
Russia, linked thus readily with the north. Such is the view
of the latest investigator (Eggers), though his principal
predecessor (Ekholm) preferred Italy.[1] There the matter
may be left until the door is open for further research.

GLASS

Under the Early Empire, glassware was not traded abundantly into Free Germany; some fourteen pieces in all can
be ascribed to the first or early second century A.D. Of these
the most abundant type is that of a ribbed or pillared bowl,
such as may be found throughout the vast zone covered
by Roman trade at that time, from Britain to India (fig. 20,
1–2, p. 188). Eight pillared bowls have been found, ranging
from Oslo to Poland, all probably or certainly in 'chieftains' graves' of the Lübsow group (p. 49). (It may be
recalled that some of the 'Chieftains' were women: a particularly fine bowl, for example, of white-marbled blue
glass was recovered from a woman's grave at Juellinge on
Laaland – see pl. 4, 3 – together with other imports, including a bronze *patera* signed by the well-known maker
L. Ansius Diodorus, who worked at or near Capua between
c. A.D. 60 and 90.) The remaining half-dozen early glasses
are conical beakers, either cut to facets or painted. An
example from one of the Lübsow graves bears two painted
zones of gladiators.

All these glass vessels probably came from Campania by
way of Carnuntum and the central European river-system.
The factories of provincial Germany belong to the Middle

1. *Acta Arch.* VI (1935), 71ff.

and Later Empire, the glass of which has recently been reviewed in detail by Eggers, with inevitable reservations as to the part played by South Russia in third- and fourth-century distributions. His maps show a great concentration in the Danish islands, especially Zealand, a fair scatter along and behind the Baltic coast as far as the eastern end of the Gulf of Danzig, a minor concentration in Thuringia, sporadic occurrences far to the south-east along the Dniester and in the Ukraine, and a notable extension towards the north in Sweden and Norway, as far north indeed as the Trondheim fiord. On the other hand, between the Elbe and the Rhine, except in Thuringia, only two determinate glass vessels of the later period have come to light, in spite of the relative proximity of the Rhenish factories. The explanation offered is doubtless in part a right one; that in the west the dominance of cremation has robbed the archaeologist of any easy source of material. Against this, however, must be set the fact that cremation was likewise prevalent in Norway, which has nevertheless proved singularly productive. Chance and archaeological skill or enterprise may be suspected as contributory factors. Paradoxically, Roman glass is completely absent from Bohemia, destined long afterwards to become itself a European centre of glass-manufacture. During the brief early period of commercial prosperity there, glass was rarely traded across the frontiers; and later, when glass became a major Roman export, Marcomannic trade had dwindled almost to extinction.

Notable amongst late types which can be ascribed to western factories are the somewhat rare cylindrical cups, painted with human figures, and those of animals, to which the name 'Nordrup-Jesendorf' has been given from find-spots respectively in Zealand and Mecklenburg (pl. 12A). Nineteen examples of this type have been found, representing eight localities, all of them accessible by the North Sea coastal route from the Rhine, with a land-traverse across the Danish peninsula. Another type which can be recognized as western by form and fabric is a small bowl with applied ribs; a type represented mostly in Thuringia with an outlier east of the Oder. Other small bowls with cut geometrical patterns, a type characteristic of Cologne, occur not only in the Danish islands, Mecklenburg, and Thuringia, but also far away amongst the tributaries of the Danube and the Theiss and northwards by the gulf of Danzig, a distribution which suggests in part a sea-route and in part a cross-country route from the upper Rhine to the Danube. We have seen that these cut-glass bowls or cups were sometimes imitated in silver (pl. 8B). Other types from Free Germany are noted by Eggers as foreign to the Rhenish factories and, with some help from geographical distribution, are ascribed provisionally to the Black Sea markets, though more positive evidence is admittedly required. Relatively tall, slim beakers with applied thread-ornaments, differing from their western counterparts both in form and in the colour and quality of their threads, occur in Zealand (pl. 10A), in the neighbourhood of the Vistula delta, and in the valley of the Dniester, and are thus attributed. They seem to belong mostly to the third century. Two other south-eastern or at least non-western types have a further interest in that they bring Norway and Sweden into the picture, presumably by way of the Dniester, San, Vistula, and Denmark. The first consists of small glass cups with claw-like ribs extending from the base half-way up the sides (pl. 12B). This late type has been found on three sites near the mouth of the Vistula, on Bornholm and Zealand, at the north end of Jutland, on two sites in southern Norway and one site in western Sweden. The other type comprises

tumblers of thick olive-green glass with cut ornament
in which sunk ovals predominate (p. 13A). In date these
tumblers come at the end of our period and overlap
that of the Folk-wandering, which their distribution in
Norway (seventeen sites) seems to herald or reflect. In this
respect they conform closely in time and place with the
'Westland' type of bronze bucket discussed above (p. 101).
For the rest the tumblers occur on two Swedish sites, in
Jutland and the Danish islands, in Pomerania, at the mouth
of the Vistula, and in the upper valley of the Oder, thus
conforming with the familiar pattern of south-central and
south-eastern Europe. Incidentally, a factor in the wide
distribution of these tumblers may have been the unusually
thick and durable glass of which they are made.

Lastly, a word must be said of the glass drinking-horns
with which Rhenish factories supplemented the metal-
mounted ox-horns of the German tradition (p. 37).
Whether the Rhenish factories exercised a monopoly in
this matter is less certain. Glass horns have been found in
inhumation-graves in Southern Norway (two), Sweden
(one), Jutland (one), Zealand (two), and East Prussia (one),
and appear to date mainly from the fourth and fifth centuries, perhaps with emphasis on the later date (pl. 13B).
The period is one in which, on present knowledge, it is
increasingly difficult to allot sources as between east and
west, and the distribution is too generalized to help. Once
again, the Iron Curtain bars the necessary research.

TERRA SIGILLATA

The ease with which the familiar red-glazed pottery known
as *terra sigillata* or 'Samian' can be recognized and roughly
dated gives it a special value to the archaeologist, and the
fact that 262 sites in Free Germany and Scandinavia have

produced sherds of it[1] brings it prominently into the present context (fig. 14). Let it be said at once, however, that a large proportion of these sites represents short-range trade to the Frisian coast or up the tributaries of the Rhine. Friesland alone accounts for not less than forty-two sites; and the limitations of the trade are emphasized by the circumstance that Denmark, in spite of a century of intensive exploration, has yielded only four examples, whilst on the Swedish island of Gotland, rich in Roman bronze vessels and not lacking in Roman glass, only one bowl of *terra sigillata* has been recorded. This solitary Gotland bowl, incidentally, offers a warning to the student. It comes from an ancient farm-settlement at Känne, on the south-eastern shore of the island, where systematic excavations were carried out in 1926–31 and produced thirty-nine sherds of decorated *sigillata* spread over an area of about four hundred square miles. The fragments cannot be made to join one another, but have been shown to represent a single bowl. It is a cautionary thought that a less careful investigation or a less distinctive vessel might easily have multiplied the distribution-density of *terra sigillata* on Gotland thirty-nine times!

The earliest *sigillata* found in Free Germany is an Arretine vessel (probably early first century A.D.) from Holtgaste, Kr. Leer, in Hanover. The extreme scarcity of Arretine or Italian ware in Free Germany is, however, in contrast with its comparative abundance in Britain (at Colchester and elsewhere) before the Roman conquest. A few specimens of early provincial *sigillata*, made in the south of Gaul between A.D. 25 and 95, have been recorded: notably a bowl of the type known as 'Dragendorff 29' from Vippa-

1. Dagmar Selling, 'Terra Sigillatafynd i det Fria Germanien', in *Kulturhistoriska Studier tillagnade Nils Aberg* (Stockholm, 1938), pp. 101–114; and a fuller list in Eggers (1951), p. 182.

chedalhausen, Kr. Weimar, in Thuringia, and a dish of form 'Dragendorff 18' stamped OF BASSI CO (i.e. the factory of Bassus and Coelus) from Mehrum near Düsseldorf, and therefore not far from the Roman frontier. Both of these

Fig. 14. Distribution of *terra sigillata*

vessels date approximately from the third quarter of the first century A.D. Another bowl, made probably at Banassac in South Gaul towards A.D. 100, has been found at Dzwinogrod, Krets Bobrka, in Poland, and is the most easterly example for which a first-century date can be claimed. It may have found its way up from Carnuntum on the Danube rather than transversely across north-central Europe.

For the rest, the *sigillata* now in question dates mostly from the second century and was derived either from Lezoux in central Gaul or from one or other of the factories which sprang up in the frontier territories from the end of the first century A.D. onwards: at Heiligenberg, Rheinzabern, Blickweiler, Trier, and Westerndorf. Thus, one of the four Danish examples (from Valløby in Zealand) is a bowl stamped by Comitialis, who worked at Rheinzabern in the middle and latter part of the second century; a decorated bowl by Cintugnatus, who was at Heiligenberg in the first half of the century, is recorded from Borstel in Saxony; another bowl (form 37) from Dortmund in Westphalia bears the name of the Trier potter Amator, of the second half of the second century; Tarvagus of Westerndorf, mid-second century, stamped a vessel from Dambitzen, Kr. Elbing, in West Prussia; sherds from Ciosmy (near Lodz) and Dzwinogrod in Poland bear the names of Elenius and Cintusmus, who worked at Rheinzabern and Westerndorf after the middle of the second century; whilst as long ago as 1776 a bowl of form thirty-seven was recorded from Gispersleben, near Erfurt in Thuringia, bearing the name of Drusus, who worked at Lezoux in the first half of the second century. A few examples of *sigillata* are decorated in barbotine and 'cut-glass' techniques, which may carry them into the third century; but, save for inferior derivatives, the manufacture of this fabric ceased after the first quarter of that century.

If we turn from date and type to distribution, certain points of interest arise. First, the terminal character of the trade with the Frisian coast and its hinterland, extending to the mouth of the Elbe, is sufficiently clear from the abundance of *sigillata* on the *terps* and its absence from the Danish peninsula. It is evident that the Frisians were in this respect absorbers rather than mere carriers. Secondly, the transfusion of wares into the valleys on the eastern flank of the middle Rhine may mostly be dismissed as petty frontier trade, but, on the other hand, some part of this traffic went further afield: up the Lippe, for example, to the Minden-Hameln crossings of the Weser, and along the Main-Fulda and Wetterau routes to the vicinity of the Thuringian Forest, where nearly twenty *sigillata* find-spots recall the considerable concentration of Roman bronze vessels and coinage hereabouts (p. 38). Thuringia indeed appears once more as a rather mysterious island of romanization *in partibus*. Thirdly, reference has been made to some slight evidence – too slight at present for emphasis – that *sigillata* occasionally reached east-central Europe and the Baltic via the amber-route from Carnuntum. Some of the German provincial potteries, notably Westerndorf, traded with the Danube frontier, and *sigillata* sherds found in Czechoslovakia (at Prodbaba, near Prague), in East Prussia near Elbing at the mouth of the Vistula, and less certainly, the Gotland (Känne) bowl already mentioned have been attributed to Westerndorf and are perhaps more likely to have travelled by way of the Danube and thence northwards than more directly eastwards from the Rhine.

CHAPTER SIX

FREE GERMANY: SUMMARY

THE previous sections have shown, if selectively, the remarkable extent to which Roman things penetrated into Free Germany between the first and fourth centuries A.D. From that summary much has been omitted; brooches,[1] for example, and pins and beads, in all of which native elements (Gaulish, Danubian, German) are mingled almost inextricably with other elements from the south and west. But detailed studies by categories or localities are not the function of this book and have indeed been supplied in liberal measure for the time being by the lists and maps of Drs Bolin and Eggers.[2] Here it must suffice to observe the general trends of the evidence which they and others have collected.

That evidence points to three main and in some degree successive sources. The first source was Italy, which in the first century A.D. and well into the second century was the manufacturer and primary distributor of most of the Roman goods found on Free German soil. Wares travelled by an adequate road-service to the Danube and thence by the amber-routes to the Baltic or, in the early part of the first century, to Bohemia. Here the Marcomanni were for a time active both as ultimate customers and as middlemen in the central and northern European trade, but after the exile of Maroboduus fell quickly out of the running. In the west, the provinces of Gaul and western Germany absorbed Italian goods and passed them on to barbarian buyers by

---

1. For these the standard work is still O. Almgren, 'Studien über nordeuropäische Fibelformen', *Mannus*, nr. 32 (Leipzig, 1923).

2. See Bibliography, p. 215 and p. 83, footnote 3.

sea and land. Trade was supplemented by diplomatic gifts to native princes, who, incidentally, sometimes reciprocated; as when the Cimbri sought to propitiate Augustus by the gift of a peculiarly sacred vessel (Strabo, 7. 2. 1). Time-expired soldiery from the Roman auxiliary forces, returning to their native homes, must have carried back with them Roman knicknacks and an appreciation of Roman things. War booty must also have contributed to the interchange, but is difficult to isolate. What the Roman traders received in return for their enterprise is almost unknown. Slaves may be assumed to have formed a part of the apparatus, although the human fruits of victory must have constituted a serious rival source. Skins may also have been included; Drusus exacted from the Frisians a tribute of ox-hides for the equipment of his army (Tacitus, *Ann.* IV, 72), and these same Frisian ranchers doubtless continued to supply hides or livestock to the neighbouring provinces. Marcus Aurelius received cattle and horses from the Quadi and others (Dio, LXXI, 11). From Scandinavia, furs and dried fish were probably traded; furs at least were widely used for clothing by the Germans, although we have no contemporary evidence for them in the present context. Amber from Jutland and the coasts of East Prussia remained a commercial objective, though whether it retained its prehistoric dominance is perhaps questionable. But, with all allowance for these obvious commodities, there is much in the apparatus of Romano-German commerce that is unknown to us and is likely to remain so. Perishable imports to Italy and the provinces must have formed a major part of it.

Attention has been drawn to the early prominence of the islands and mainland of Denmark in this traffic, and it has been suspected that their prominence reflects some measure of political cohesion, probably with Zealand as its

focus. Whether, or how far, piracy may have contributed
to this accession of wealth in the western Baltic can only
be guessed, but in any case some more regular form of
exploitation – doubtless including control of amber agencies – must be added.

How far Italy remained a source of supply after the
earlier part of the second century is difficult to say. Our
knowledge of Italian factories in the Middle and Later
Empire lacks precision, and the routes across the Danube
may have continued to contribute more than we know.
Certainly, however, by the end of the second century the
second main source of supply had come into operation:
Gaul and the Rhineland. Pottery, glass, metalware, and
coinage now began to flow thence eastwards and north-
eastwards, encouraged alike by prosperity in the west and
by central European wars and migrations which, from the
time of Marcus Aurelius, must have slowed down such
direct Italian traffic as remained. Here and there an attempt
has been made to trace the impact of tribal movement in
the map-pattern of Roman commodities, especially coin-
hoards, but with very uncertain success. The astonishing
bog-hoards of the third and fourth centuries are presumably, however, the product of victories or successful forays
on the fringes of the Empire, and again emphasize the
dominance of the Danish lands.

The third main source is assumed without close docu-
mentation to have been based on Graeco-Scythian South
Russia, with extension to Byzantium. Much further research, not at present feasible, is required before the share
of the factories and markets of this region can be adequately
appraised. Meanwhile, it is rather on negative than on
positive evidence that certain categories of glass and metalwork from Free Germany are ascribed to the link established by the Goths in and after the third century between

the Baltic and the Black Sea. This link was later supplemented by the impact of the Goths and Huns upon the Empire itself. The phase lies outside the scope of the present book; otherwise it might have been fitting to distinguish Byzantium as a fourth source rather than as a supplement to the third. The great quantities of Imperial gold which now found their way to the southern shore and eastern islands of the Baltic indicate the trends of the time. It may indeed be that, when the contemporary historian Priscus affirms that Attila the Hun ruled 'the islands in the Ocean', those of Bornholm, Öland, and Gotland are intended,[1] and that the numerous gold *solidi* found there represent the ultimate diffusion of plunder or tribute from the Byzantine Emperor. For example, in A.D. 435 Attila was able to impose upon the Eastern Empire an annual tribute of 700 lb of gold, and seven years later the annual levy was increased to 2,100 lb. Established by such means on a vicarious Gold Standard, east-central and Baltic Europe poised glittering upon the brink of one of the dramatically·formative periods of history.

A final comment may be added. What, on the broadest and longest view, was the historical significance of this penetration of wares, often of a high grade, far into the interior of barbarian Europe during more than four centuries? Is the study of them merely the laborious collection of *disjecta*, of cultural accidents and curiosities out of context? I think not. They played in fact a very positive part in history. They are milestones on the barbarian road to El Dorado. The subsequent literature of Northern Europe makes abundantly clear the fascination which the Empire exercised upon the minds of those without it. The Empire was the Promised Land, of wealth untold and of

1. See E. A. Thompson, *A History of Attila and the Huns* (Oxford, 1948), p. 76.

perennial allure. Large-scale migration is commonly attributable to economic and social factors based on climatic change, soil-exhaustion, unbalanced population, changing markets, political encroachment. But to these propelling causes which lie behind migration must be added others which lie in front of it, attract it, or stimulate it. To barbarian Europe, at least from the middle of the second century onwards, the Empire was in the latter category. Marcomanni, Franks, Alamanni, Burgundians, Vandals, Goths, whatever involuntary rearward forces propelled them, at least knew well where they were going. Traders and raiders and perhaps returning conscripts or mercenaries had already demonstrated the way to fortune. The commodities which we have catalogued marked out the highroads of great folk-movements and advertised along them the delights which lay ahead. Only when at the end of the fourth century the Huns of Asia entered abruptly into the European scene were the main lines of barbarian enterprise bent rudely from the traditional objective. A wedge was now driven deeply into European migration; and thenceforth the tribes of northern Germany and Scandinavia, cut off from the sun, turned their faces with a new determination to the mists of the North Sea. We leave them there and turn our own faces to the far south.

PART TWO: AFRICA

CHAPTER SEVEN

THE SAHARA

In recent years the Roman occupation of Algeria and Libya has been the subject of illuminating researches carried out on the ground and from the air by French, Italian and British explorers.[1] These researches require co-ordination and extension, but meanwhile our picture of the organization of the provinces of Numidia (embracing southern Algeria, Tunisia, and Tripolitania) and Cyrenaica has acquired a new actuality, and coherent maps are for the first time available. The present is not the context for a review of this evidence. It will suffice here to indicate certain general features by way of introduction to a more ample notice of discoveries in the deserts beyond the frontier zone.

The mountainous geography of Algeria diversified the settlement of the countryside to a greater extent than did the broader natural partitions of Libya, and at the same time, by canalizing traffic, invited a more definitive system of frontier control. That control was based, perhaps from the time of Hadrian in the twenties and thirties of the second century A.D., on an intermittent artificial barrier of varying design some 500 miles long, linking natural obstacles of mountain and salt-marsh and cutting the

1. See particularly J. Baradez, *Fossatum Africae* (Paris, 1949); R. G. Goodchild and J. B. Ward Perkins, 'The *Limes Tripolitanus* in the Light of Recent Discoveries', *Journ. Roman Studies*, xxxix (1949), 81ff.; R. G. Goodchild, 'The *Limes Tripolitanus*: ii', *ib.* xl (1950), 30ff.

approaches into the province from the south-west. The
defences were reorganized by the Emperor Septimius
Severus, himself of African origin, and he or his successors
added a buffer zone by the establishment of *coloni* (controlled cultivators) outside a part of the frontier line. Apart
from this specific act there is no doubt that a large share in
the defence of the frontier was still delegated as late as the
beginning of the fifth century to the native farmers, who
as remains of fields and irrigation works show, were settled
abundantly in its vicinity. Details of this native occupation,
whether inside or close outside the barrier, are at present inadequately known and in any event do not concern us here.

Further east, however, the situation was at the same time
clearer and less closely defined. Libya falls naturally from
north to south into three or four roughly parallel zones:
the coastal plain, the broken rocky plateau or *gebel* (considerable areas of which are comparatively well-watered and
were in Roman times covered with olive plantations), and
a belt of stony desert, broken by seasonal water-courses,
and best designated as steppe, merging finally into the
landscape of the Sahara. The first was inevitably the land
of the considerable colonial cities, Carthaginian or Greek
in origin, later enlarged and supplemented by Imperial
commerce. The second and third were the lands of semi-
nomadic pastoralists and cultivators, whom it was a task of
Rome to anchor both as producers and as a first-line militia.
The fourth was the limitless reservoir of nomadic enemies
to all that the settled societies of the Mediterranean stood
for. Had a fixed frontier barrier, a wall or a ditch, been
envisaged, it must have stood between the third and fourth
of these zones. But the absence of easy tactical command
on the fringe of the desert would have made a huge line
of this sort both costly to build and impossibly costly to
maintain and defend. Instead, the frontier zone was patrolled

by occasional vexillations or detachments of the Third Augustan Legion (until its disbandment in A.D. 238) and, at least from the beginning of the third century, by bands of local irregulars. Under the Later Empire, however, defence crystallized primarily into a static complex of fortified farms or *gasrs* (*gsur*) in which the farmers of the *gebel* and the steppe increasingly barricaded themselves and so, incidentally and somewhat uncertainly, barricaded the province. Analogy is presented partially by the Scottish *brochs* or fortified farmsteads of the Romano-British period; more closely, by the pele towers maintained by the yeomen of the Anglo-Scottish border-lands in the Middle Ages.

Through this miscellaneous frontier belt the cities of the coastal fringe received, in varying degrees, the products of the African interior. Ivory, precious stones, gold-dust, ostrich feathers, slaves are mentioned or inferred, and, above all, animals for the amphitheatres of Rome and elsewhere. Some of these commodities were obtainable within the provinces themselves, but some must have come from further afield, transported by the caravans which were the principal asset of the desert nomads. A French historian has indeed remarked that, if Amsterdam be said to have been founded on herring-bones, Lepcis Magna, the great trading city on the Tripolitanian coast, may be said to have been built on the carcases of camels – though olive-stones might have been historically more correct! The proviso should in any case be added that there is no certain evidence for the normal use of the camel in the coastal tracts before the third century A.D.

THE FEZZAN

The Roman markets most accessible to this long-range caravan trade were the three which gave Tripolitania

(Land of the Three Cities) its name: from west to east,
Sabratha, Oea (now the town of Tripoli), and Lepcis Magna
itself, all set in a southward re-entrant of the Mediterranean.
It was no accident that the hardy column which, under
General Leclerc, struggled through from Lake Chad to the
sea in 1943 made the coast at Tripoli. Whether the west
coast or central Africa were the ultimate goal, the traveller
from the Mediterranean would usually make his way
southwards to the east-west ridge which forms the spine
of the Sahara from the Hoggar on the west to Tibesti on
the east, and would tend to travel along it, one way or
another, rather than engulf himself in the boundless sand-
plateau at its foot. And, appropriately enough, midway
between that ridge and the coastal plain, in the Fezzan
430 miles (in a straight line) south of Lepcis Magna, a
remarkable assemblage of Roman things was brought to
light in 1933-4 by an Italian mission led by Professor Pace
in association with Dr Caputo and Professor Sergi.[1] The
mission was in the field for little more than three months,
and its results testify alike to the energy of its directors and
the abundance of the material.

The region in question lies some fifty miles north of
Murzuch, one of the capitals of the Fezzan, and is itself
bounded on the north by the Wadi el-Agial, which runs
east and west by way of Germa, the ancient Garama,
known to Pliny as 'the celebrated capital of the Garamantes' (v, 36). To the north of the *wadi* (seasonal water-
course, dry for the greater part of the year) lies the sand-sea,
practically devoid of life; to the south a strip of stony
plateau, the *hammada*, rises to a range of hills, and offers a
milieu suitable for Berber occupation. Here, between Tin

1. *Monumenti Antichi*, XLI (Rome, 1951), cols. 151-552. Objects
brought back by the expedition are in the Museo Coloniale in
Rome.

Abunda on the west and El-Abiad on the east – a distance of about a hundred miles – the expedition identified many thousands of ancient graves distributed in groups along the plain and foot-hills. Other evidences of settlement in the area, though less abundant superficially, are not absent. The seasonal rains of the *hammada* were collected and controlled on a considerable scale by embanked canals and subterranean galleries which presumably represent a skill imported from within the Roman provinces of the north (see p. 120). Actual habitations are at present little known, but a stone-walled 'promontory-fort' commands the *wadi* half a dozen miles south-west of Germa, and a few simple square-roomed dwellings are recorded. These various structures are ascribed tentatively to the time of the Roman Empire, and a house partially excavated at Germa itself is more certainly of third-century date, though with Byzantine repairs.

Of the graves, a majority are cairns, either of roughly heaped stones or revetted on a rectangular plan with careful dry-stone walling, sometimes plastered, and with a crudely domed or pyramidal top. The burial chamber within had in some cases been corbel-vaulted with rough rubble-masonry. In front of the tomb was occasionally a bath-like offering-table of stone, with a main oblong cavity and smaller compartments along one of the edges. With these tables might be associated low *stelae*, which sometimes bifurcate into two projections resembling horns. Inhumation was the rule, and the skeleton was flexed with varying orientation. But in the present context the important feature of the graves is less their structural form than the fact that not a few of them include pottery, glass, and lamps of Roman origin (pl. 10B). Here a few examples must suffice.

About three miles east of the Germa mausoleum, of which something will be said later, is a cemetery containing a notable tomb of the plastered square or oblong type already mentioned. It had been surmounted by a stepped pyramid, preserved to a maximum height of 4½ ft, with two bicorn *stelae* on the first step of the eastern end. Within was a rubble-faced burial chamber of trapezoidal plan, 8 × 10½ × 10 × 7½ ft, with a depth of 6 ft. The tomb had been broken into previously, the bones scattered and the grave-goods smashed. Nevertheless, the following fragments indicated the former richness of the equipment: two Roman clay lamps of late third- or early fourth-century date; a cylindrical glass bottle with incised square panels, probably of the third century; a green glass cup decorated with simple blue spots alternating with triangular groups of smaller blue spots, a type also of the late third or early fourth century; a cylindrical beaker of similar fabric; parts of a green glass vessel bearing Greek letters; other scraps of glass, a stone roundel or gaming-counter, and two pottery cups with incised rectilinear patterns picked out in yellow, orange, and white colours. The pottery cups are non-Roman, but whether of local manufacture is less certain. The Greek lettering suggests without proving an Alexandrian origin for at least one of the glass vessels. The quantity of these in a single grave is remarkable, and indicates a fairly close contact between the Fezzan and the Mediterranean about A.D. 300 or a little later.

A similar but rather larger tomb nearby was of the same general date, and produced further examples of the non-Roman polychrome ware, together with beads and a bone comb, and with lamps, amphorae, a glass beaker, and other objects from the Mediterranean world. A third tomb of the group was even more amply furnished and was probably that of a lady of rank. It was of plastered, dry-built masonry and retained two steps of a pyramid surmounting a rectangular base about 24½ × 22½ ft on plan. Immediately east of the tomb was a stone offering table of the kind described above, with the remains of two bicorn *stelae*. Amongst the contents were five red-glazed plates (possibly of the second century A.D.), two amphorae, and several plates and cups of cut or moulded glass, one bearing a fragmentary Greek inscription restored on analogy as Κα[λως] πιε, 'Drink well' or 'Your good health'. More notable are fragments of woollen cloth which possibly represent a purse, and lay on a stone plate in the south-west angle of the tomb. The cloth had been variegated with geometric patterns in yellow, red, and blue colours on a purple ground, and was clearly an imported fabric of some value; it may be recalled that dye factories along the African coast are mentioned by Strabo (17. 3. 18) and were doubtless an inheritance from the Carthaginians. The tomb also preserved by chance in its plaster the matrices of two hammers with stone heads bound on to hafts by thongs. Altogether, the equipment was of mixed character and date, but would appear to have been assembled early in the fourth century.

In the immediate vicinity of the Germa mausoleum (see below), extensive cemeteries of somewhat poorer type, with roughly stone-lined pit-graves, produced other imports, including amphorae, *terra sigillata* of the first century, glass, and clay lamps. Two of the lamps bear the maker's name IUNI ALEXI (Junius Alexius), whose wares are widely distributed in Italy and elsewhere and are predominantly of the second century. Another, on the other hand, is of a type common to the third and fourth centuries. Such products occur in sufficient quantity to minimize the survival factor, and it may be affirmed that wares from the Roman world were freely reaching the Germa region from the end of the first to the fourth century A.D. or later, with emphasis perhaps on the third century.

Similar contacts, if (so far as is known) in lesser quantity, have been detected elsewhere along the line of the *wadi* for many miles east of Germa; and far away at Gat, over 200 miles to the south-west, a cemetery of something like 100 ruined cairns has yielded to cursory examination several glass vessels to which a third-century date may be ascribed: notably, an exceptional polychrome beaker decorated with friezes and panels representing a vine tendril, a wreath, and birds and baskets, probably of East Mediterranean (Alexandrian or Syrian) workmanship.

But at least as remarkable as these fragile imports in the heart of the Fezzan is the famous mausoleum of Germa already mentioned, by far the most southerly monument of Roman type in Africa (pl. 14). It stands alone in the desert, in its trim, classical dignity defiant of the featureless barbarism around it. It was first described by an English traveller in 1826, and, in spite of its remoteness, has often enough been visited since that date. Time and tomb-robbers have dealt drastically with the structure and its former internal arrangements are doubtful, but externally it constituted a tiny shrine with an eastern portico now represented by fragmentary columns and Ionic capitals which, with the gable-ends of the roof, lie scattered on the adjacent desert. The main body of the shrine had at each corner a sketchy angle-pilaster defined by the base and 'composite' capital carved firmly if crudely upon the quoins; it is possible that the shafts of the pilasters were originally indicated in plaster. The base of the three-stepped pedestal on which the building stands is about 12 × 10 ft and the height to the top of the cornice is 15 ft. The ashlar blocks are excellently squared and fitted, and, save for a provincialism in its carving, the monument might have graced one of the great coastal cities.

The expedition of 1933 dug out the interior to the natural

soil, and found in the course of their work fragments of several Roman lamps of the first or early second century A.D., glass of various colours, Italian red-glazed ware of a type ascribed to the end of the first century, and sherds of less determinate red and white ware, together with rough sherds and knives of flint and obsidian of 'neolithic' aspect though presumably contemporary with the other objects. The occurrence of obsidian is of interest, since its nearest source appears to be in the Mediterranean islands, Pantelleria, Lipari, and Santorin. The architectural character of the monument, its contents where datable, and the general period of the adjacent burials are all consistent with a date in the latter part of the first century.

The adjacent burials referred to lie less than one yard to the west of the mausoleum and consist of two graves under a heap of sand and stones, each grave containing a Roman amphora of the first-second-century type with burnt bones. These two cremation-burials in a region in which the rite is otherwise that of inhumation are significant, particularly in view of their proximity to the mausoleum; it cannot be doubted that they, like the monument itself, represent the intrusion of visitors from the Roman world, where at this time cremation was the normal mode.

For the rest, description may here be confined to one other monument. A short distance to the south of the mausoleum are the ruins of a rectangular dry-stone building about 70 × 40 ft externally with two compartments entered through the eastern wall. The eastern compartment was probably a court; the western contained a dry-built stone tomb, square on plan with rounded corners and formerly roofed as a truncated pyramid. Externally against the front of the tomb were six rough *stelae* or orthostats about 2 ft high, and again in front of them, in the entrance through the cross-wall, which was of unbaked brick, was a carefully cut oblong stone trough or offering-table nearly 5 ft in length, flanked by two circular stone basins, with a third shallow basin to the east. Burnt bones of sheep and oxen, mixed with sherds of wheel-turned pottery, were encountered in great quantity by the excavators, particularly against the cross-wall, and there were numerous hearths, and at one point a flint knife. In and around the tomb were groups of votive pots, mostly amphorae (sometimes incised with Berber letters) but also sherds of red ware, with a stone handmill and a pillared blue glass bowl of a well-known first-century type. These objects extended in depth through an appreciable accumulation of soil and were thought to represent a series of successive deposits and a considerable length of time. Amongst the surface-finds was a fragment of an Italian *sigillata* bowl bearing the head of Diana, and perhaps of late first- or second-century date.

This remarkable assemblage, with its distinctive plan and imported wares, would appear to represent a long-lived funerary shrine, of a lower technical grade altogether than the mausoleum, but of a kind derived also from the north and rooted perhaps in Carthaginian rather than in Roman tradition. The extent, however, if any, to which the Fezzan ritual, with its *baetyls* or *stelae* and offering-tables, should be affiliated to Carthaginian practice must remain undecided until far more is known than at present of the ritual of the Punic colonies themselves.

So much for the archaeological evidence as it stands at present from the Fezzan. That it should fit easily or exactly into the episodic history of that region in the time of the Empire is almost too much to hope; nevertheless, the salient historical facts are worth recalling. In 19 B.C. the pro-consul Cornelius Balbus celebrated a triumph after a successful punitive expedition against the Garamantes whose homeland it was, and their capital Garama is mentioned by Pliny amongst the cities which he captured. There is a faint echo of a similar campaign, undated, against the Marmaridae further east; and both enterprises may be seen as moments in the age-long struggle between the settled civilization of the Mediterranean littoral and the nomads or semi-nomads of the mountain and the desert. The antagonism, being of deep-rooted social rather than political origin, was almost incapable of solution, and, in spite of intermittent negotiation, the restless opportunism of the tribesmen long continued to ensure their participation in any trouble that might be afoot. Thus in A.D. 69 a domestic dispute between the coastal cities of Oea (Tripoli) and Lepcis Magna led to the entry of the Garamantes on the part of Oea and the devastation of the countryside up to the walls of Lepcis. The incident was the occasion of the second major Roman expedition into the interior, led this time by the proconsul Valerius Festus, who followed, we are told, a 'short route of only four days' and cannot therefore, at the best, have penetrated far into the tribal area. Writing shortly after the Oea incident, however, Pliny speaks of the Fezzan tribe as 'subjugated', although it would appear that further punitive expeditions were needed to confirm the hasty retaliation of Festus. At any rate, by the end of the first or the beginning of the second century opportunity or necessity had evidently swung the Garamantes towards the established rule, for Ptolemy the geographer records two exploratory ventures through their territory (I, 8, 4-5). The date of these ventures is not given, but they must have occurred between the time of Pliny (died A.D. 79) and that of Ptolemy (about A.D. 150). On the first occasion, Septimius Flaccus marched with troops to Garama and proceeded thence southwards for three months into 'the midst of the Aethiopians', a circumstance which suggests vague inquiry rather than a measured campaign. The second venture was led by an otherwise unknown Julius Maternus, under what auspices is not recorded. Maternus set out from Lepcis Magna and came to Garama, whence, with the co-operation of the king of the Garamantes, he led his expedition towards the south for four months against the 'Aethiopians' and reached the unidentified country of Agisymba, 'where the rhinoceri are wont to assemble'.[1] Both of these enterprises were doubtless designed, at least in part, to secure information at source regarding commodities such as ivory, precious woods, and Aethiopian slaves, familiar to the Roman world through middlemen whose interest it was to preserve trade secrets and sustain prices. Of these middlemen the Garamantes must have been amongst the chief, and the archaeological evidence summarized above suggests that they continued to profit from their position for two centuries or more after the recorded missions.

A review of that evidence in the light of the historical episodes suggests a certain measure of agreement between the two. The Roman imports in the homeland of the Garamantes appear to begin at the end of the first century A.D. – that is, precisely at the time when a sufficiently durable *rapprochement* was first established between the Empire and the Fezzani nomads. The direct interest of the Roman world in the desert and beyond, expressed historically by the journeys of Flaccus and Maternus, is expressed archaeologically by the Germa mausoleum, which presumably commemorates a Roman agent and his companions or successors established at the Garamantian capital with the goodwill of the king. It was thus that at an earlier date

1. For an interesting discussion of these expeditions in their geographical context, see F. Rennell Rodd, *People of the Veil* (London, 1926), pp. 322ff.

Roman pioneers had settled far beyond the northern frontier at the capital of the Marcomanni in Bohemia with the goodwill of Maroboduus (pp. 23 and 37). But it may be that another analogy is in fact more apt to the Fezzan episode. Within a decade or two of the erection of the Germa monument, Domitian was attempting to quieten the formidable Decebalus, king of the Dacians in central Europe, by sending him money 'and artisans of every trade, both peaceful and warlike' (p. 24). Is a similar policy manifest at Germa, not only in the presence of this surprising monument, but also and above all in the impressive irrigation systems of the *hammada* by the Wadi el-Agial? The date of these is unknown, but it is difficult to dissociate them from the phase of Roman contact. A primary object of the Roman provinces along the Mediterranean littoral must have been to anchor the predatory nomads, who, on their swift camels, were a proved menace from the deserts of the south. How better to anchor them than by turning them into food-producers, by teaching them to till their own deserts? To the military pacification momentarily effected under the Flavian emperors, a systematic instruction in agricultural engineering was a proper long-term sequel. It is perhaps as likely therefore that the Germa mausoleum represents a Romano-Libyan agricultural technician or adviser who died on a mission to the court of the Garamantes, as that it represents an enterprising commercial agent or a member of what we to-day would call the consular service.

Be that as it may, the evidences of trade are likewise sufficiently apparent in the archaeological record which has been summarized above. The question arises, What was its material basis? What did the Garamantian caravans deliver to the coastal cities in exchange for the wine, the pottery, the cloth, and above all the varied glassware which these remote people prized and buried with their dead?

Gold-dust, ostrich eggs and feathers, ivory, precious stones and woods, animals, slaves have been lightly mentioned, but it must be admitted that specific historical evidence is of the slightest. Strabo at the end of the first century B.C. tells us that 'the land . . . of the Garamantes . . . is the land whence the Carthaginian Stones [i.e. carbuncles] are brought' (17. 3. 18), and Pliny nearly a century later has a similar story (v. 34). Elephants from the African jungle were familiar, in art if not in life, to every Roman schoolboy.[1] A component of glass, natron or carbonate of soda, is said to occur in the Fezzan and *may* have been exported thence in exchange for the finished products. But it is best to admit that, like the equivalent problem in Free Germany, the economic problem of the penetration of Roman things into desert Africa is only partially solved. It is worth noting as a likely analogy that in the Middle Ages, until the Portuguese tapped its source from their new settlements in the Gulf of Guinea, gold dust came from the Sudan by the trade-routes of the Sahara to the coastal cities from Tripoli to Ceuta, where merchants from Italy and Spain sustained a flourishing traffic.[2]

Of the routes by which the trade was operated, and indeed of the routes followed by the Roman military expeditions into the Fezzan, it can only be said that there are three principal possibilities with a considerable choice of variants. A westerly track led from Sabratha on the coast south-westwards to Ghadames, the ancient Cydamus, near the Tunisian border and thence south-eastwards to the

1. See generally S. Aurigemma, 'L'elefante di Leptis Magna', *Rivista Africa Italiana*, VII (1940), 67ff.

2. F. M. Powicke, *Three lectures given in the Hall of Balliol College, Oxford* (Oxford, 1947), pp. 58–9, citing Fernand Brandel, 'Monnaies et civilisations: De l'or du Sudan á l'argent d'Amérique', in *Annales: économies, sociétés, civilisations*, I (1946), 9–22.

heart of the Fezzan. An easterly track passed from Lepcis Magna through Beni Ulid and Bu Ngem (perhaps the ancient Vanias) to Hun, at the foot of the Gebel es-Soda, which has been identified with the ancient Mons Ater or Niger, and thence southwards to the Fezzan. Between these was a more direct route from Oea (Tripoli) via Mizda and Gheria. This central track, as is shown by milestones along it, was much used in the third century A.D. if not earlier. In the absence, however, of relevant archaeological evidence, attempts to allot the recorded expeditions to individual routes are of no value.

TIN HINAN

So much for the Fezzan. Elsewhere the desert offers yet another problem of a more individual and elusive kind. Nearly 1,000 miles south of Algiers the mountainous backbone of the Sahara ends in the volcanic massif of the Hoggar, to which the cliché 'Mountains of the Moon' might aptly be attached. The emphatic, jagged peaks and craters in their barren setting at the same time repel and fascinate: forming a theatrical background to a strange, lonely tomb which will remain a mystery unresolved.

At the western foot of the massif, not far from the oasis of Abalessa, a rounded hill rises some 125 ft above the junction of two *wadis*. Its slopes are strewn with rocky debris from the remarkable ruin which occupies its summit. The ruin, pear-shaped on plan with a major axis of about 88 ft, resembles nothing so much as a stone-walled Scottish dun (fig. 15, p. 134). Its dry-built curtain wall varies in thickness from $4\frac{1}{2}$ to $11\frac{1}{2}$ ft, and it contains 11 rooms or courts, roughly oblong save where they conform with the rounded curtain, and standing to a height of about 6 ft. In the eastern wall is a simple entrance 5 ft wide. Large

Fig. 15. Plan of the 'palace' and tomb of Tin Hinan

iron nails and fragments of charred wood presumably represent the roofing.

The structure was clearly a small fort or fortified residence – palace would be a grandiose term. It has impressed itself upon the minds of the local Tuaregs, and their traditional story has been recorded. Long ago, we are told, there came to the Hoggar from the remote Tafilalet a lady of noble birth named Tin Hinan, accompanied by a faithful woman attendant, Takamat, and a number of slaves. The reason for her journey is not stated, and indeed does not greatly matter. She rode on a superb white camel, and brought with her from the land of the Berbers several loads of dates and millet. But the way to the Hoggar was long, and hunger began to menace the caravan; until one day the resourceful Takamat saw a number of anthills and, dismounting, proceeded to rob the ants of their laboriously stored grain. Thus fortified, they eventually reached the Hoggar, and in some fashion not elaborated Tin Hinan there became the ancestress of the Tuareg nobility. The structure now in question is her monument.[1]

Excavations in 1926 and again in 1933 produced astonishing results. Room number one, in the south-western corner of the complex, had been turned into a tomb-chamber or, rather, tomb-antechamber. Its two doorways had been blocked up, and in the floor a number of large flat slabs covered a basement-cell about $7\frac{1}{2} \times 4\frac{1}{2}$ ft on plan and 5 ft deep which was the actual grave. In it lay the skeleton of the traditional first queen of the Hoggar, Tin Hinan. The bones, now with the other relics from

1. For this and an alternative legend, and for the monument itself, see E. F. Gautier and M. Reygasse, 'Le monument de Tin-Hinan', *Annales de l'Académie des Sciences coloniales*, VII (Paris, 1934), and M. Reygasse, *Monuments funéraires préislamiques de l'Afrique du Nord* (Paris, 1950), 88ff.

the site in the Musée du Bardo at Algiers, have been pronounced to be those of a white woman 'strongly recalling the Egyptian type of the Pharaonic monuments, the type of the upper classes, characterized by height, slenderness, wide shoulders, narrow hips, and slim legs'. Of that description, all that can be said is that it gallantly meets the demands of the legend.

No less can be said of the other contents of the grave. At the foot of the walls were fragments of matting, in the centre the remains of a bed or couch of carved wood on which lay the skeleton, slightly flexed and facing east, with powdery 'fragments of red leather' which may indicate that the body had been rouged in accordance with a wide-spread custom. On the right arm were eight bead bracelets of silver, on the left seven of gold; at the left shoulder a small stone cup contained ochre, and by it a little bundle of plants; on the breast lay a gold pendant and beads, white and red, of agate, amazonite, calcedony, carnelian, and glass. Behind the head and round the neck and shoulders were about 100 barrel-shaped silver beads, and at the left hip were some thirty other stone beads of various colours. The right foot was surrounded by beads of antimony, and beads of stone and metal were beside the left foot. At the left shoulder, cloth which fell into dust on discovery had perhaps been pinned by two iron pins. Nearby were baskets containing dates and grain, together with two wooden milk-bowls, traces of a coin of Constantine the Great, a gold ring, two small gold balls, fragments of glass with cut geometric pattern of third-fourth-century type, and a pendant of polished gypsum representing in stylized form a grotesquely developed female, obviously worn as a fertility-charm. In this mixed assemblage, the Constantinian coin and the glass indicate a fourth-century date and some now undefinable contact with the Mediterranean. The

beads are of a rudimentary kind which occurs anywhere
from the Ivory Coast to Carthage. The charm is of a
widespread class without close specific analogy. The legend
of Tin Hinan does not yield to archaeology.

Elsewhere in the little fortress the excavators found a
pottery lamp of third-century Roman type (pl. 11A),
fragments of another, a bracelet of twisted iron and another
of bronze, more beads, barbed arrowheads of iron and an
iron knife. On some of the wall-stones are fragments of
undeciphered Tifinagh inscriptions,[1] in part mutilated by
the cutting of the rough masonry and therefore earlier
than the building; and at one point a camel and another
animal are scratched on an interior surface.

Round about are several small tombs of the so-called
'chouchet' type – that is to say, a shallow pit-grave surrounded by a circular dry-built wall which derives its
name from a supposed resemblance to the *chechia* or Zouave
cap. They contain inhumations, but no grave-goods, and
merely testify to the sanctity of the site.

In the absence of comparable relics within hundreds of
miles of Tin Hinan, it is impossible at present to put her
fortlet and tomb into a wider context. The Fezzan is the
nearest known spot whence Roman goods such as the lamp
and glass could have been obtained, but reason – if such be
expected for an isolated occurrence – is lacking. To postulate that the structure may have been a rather superior
blockhouse upon a supposititious trade-route is a mere
guess. We may be content to leave Tin Hinan in geographical suspense midway between the Roman provinces
and Timbuctoo, and to think of her, perhaps, as a Lady
Hester Stanhope of another age.

1. The term Tifinagh is used for these characters by the Tuareg,
who are themselves unable to read them.

CHAPTER EIGHT

EAST AFRICA

In the latter half of the first century A.D. an anonymous Roman subject from Egypt, possibly from Berenice on the Red Sea coast, sailed the Red Sea and the Indian Ocean in merchant ships and, for the instruction of his kind, set down in unscholastic Greek a factual and remarkable account of the busy trafficking of those parts. His book, the *Periplus of the Erythraean Sea*, is a social and geographical landmark of the first order; I should describe it, indeed, as one of the most fascinating books that have come down to us from antiquity. It will be cited extensively in Chapter Nine. Here it is relevant to note the author's knowledge—somewhat vaguer, be it admitted, than usual—of the east coast of Africa, from the mouth of the Red Sea to Zanzibar, and to remark how little his lead has been followed up by archaeological investigation. Turning southward from the Cape of Spices (Cape Guardafui), he takes us in succession to the seaport of Opone (Ras Hafun?), the anchorages of Sarapion and Nikon, the Pyralaae islands, the island of Menouthias (Zanzibar?) and finally the market-port of Rhapta. (The knowledge of Ptolemy in the second century extended over 400 miles further south, probably to Cape Delgado.) The name Rhapta the *Periplus* derives from the *rhapta ploiaria*, boats sewn together with string, anciently a widespread mode of ship-construction which still survives, for example, along the coasts of southern India. The location of the town is uncertain, but is presumably within a reasonable range of Dar-es-Salaam. The interesting information is added that the native ruler of the coast hereabouts had delegated some special measure of authority to the distant trading-town of Muza, near the mouth of the Red

Sea, and that Muza sent thither 'many large ships, using Arab captains and agents who are familiar with the natives and intermarry with them and know the region and understand the language'. This was evidently a survival from the pre-Augustan era, when ocean trade was still largely in the hands of middlemen, amongst whom Arabs predominated.

The exports from these east African stations to the Roman world included, we are told, ivory, rhinoceros horn, tortoise-shell ('in best demand after that from India'), palm-oil, cinnamon, frankincense, and slaves, 'which are brought to Egypt in increasing numbers'. In return the African markets received 'lances made at Muza especially for this trade, hatchets, daggers, awls, and various kinds of glass; and at some places a little wine and wheat, not for trade but to secure the good-will of the savages'. The apparatus of African trade, whether lances or muskets, wine or gin, altered very little through the ages! Incidentally, the cinnamon recorded as an African product was probably in fact supplied by Indian traders. The *Periplus* affirms that the African seaports were in contact, not only with Egypt, but also with India, whence ships regularly brought 'wheat, rice, *ghee* [clarified butter], sesame oil, muslin, girdles, and sugar'. Some of the Indian ships discharged their cargoes actually in the African ports, but others transhipped them at sea – a practice due perhaps to the jealous exclusiveness of Arab middlemen, but more probably to the enterprise of Arab traders attempting to forestall competition ashore.

Material relics of this far-flung east coast commerce are at present almost completely lacking. The most substantial record comes from Port Durnford, 250 miles northeast of Mombasa, where Captain C. W. Waywood found in 1912 'a walled-in fortress, enclosing about five acres of

ground. He caused his native servants to dig over the top-
soil in places and was rewarded with the discovery of the
following copper coins.'[1] The list comprises one Ptolemaic (third-first century B.C.), one each of Nero and
Trajan, two of Hadrian, one of Antoninus Pius, one uncertain but of the first-second century A.D., and seemingly
seventy-nine of the fourth century A.D., amongst which
coins of Constantine I and II and Constans are mentioned.
The significance of the discovery is not necessarily vitiated
by the addition of six coins of the Mamelukes of Egypt
and seven of Egypt under the Turks (seventeenth and
eighteenth centuries). The place may well have been a
port of call from Egypt at many different periods, and is
certainly worthy of fresh examination. The Rev. Gervase
Mathew, in a letter to the writer, describes it from personal knowledge as 'an almost land-locked harbour on
the Indian Ocean, a very suitable waiting-place for the
monsoon to India, and on my reckoning the 'Nikon' of
the *Periplus*'. There for the moment this alluring problem
must be left.

For the rest, stray Roman coins and even one suspiciously
comprehensive hoard have been allegedly found between
the Sudan and the Cape.[2] In most instances the record is
inadequate or suggests a modern date for the deposit.
Nevertheless, there can be no doubt that fully authentic
deposits of the kind await discovery both along the coast
and in the hinterland when East African archaeology shall
have a mind for these matters. Meanwhile we must attend
the emergence of a worthy archaeological successor to the
adventurous Greek.

1. H. Mattingly in *Numismatic Chronicle*, 5th series, XII (London,
1932), 175.
2. M. P. Charlesworth in *Num. Chron.*, 6th series, IX (1949),
107.

PART THREE: ASIA

CHAPTER NINE

THE PERIPLUS

In the previous chapter reference was made to the Greek merchant's handbook known as the *Periplus of the Erythraean Sea*, and an outline of its contents must now be given as a preface to a consideration of Roman enterprise in the Indian sub-continent. Strabo, Pliny, Tacitus, Ptolemy the Geographer, the map known as the Peutinger Table, and the Ravenna Geographer all add materially to the definition of the picture and picturesque sidelights are thrown from the less factual literature of India itself; but were all these auxiliary sources lost to us, the *Periplus* would still preserve a clear and comprehensive outline of Rome's remarkable commerce with the East.

By the 'Erythraean' or 'Red' Sea the writer means, not merely the sea now known by that name, but all the seas traversed by this Oriental trade: the Indian Ocean, the Arabian Sea, the Persian Gulf, and even the Bay of Bengal. His knowledge often has the actuality of personal experience and, though now and then it fades apparently into hearsay, its general accuracy is unimpeachable. He begins by describing the commercial harbours of the Red Sea (in the modern usage), and notes Myos Hormos and Berenice 'both at the boundary of Egypt' as ports 'designated' for some special function[1] which is not specified – perhaps as the authorized channels for certain types of goods. Further south on the same western coast was the important port of

1. See J. A. B. Palmer in *The Classical Quarterly* N.S., I (1951), 156ff.

Adulis, which also had special legal privileges. From Pliny (*N.H.* vi, 103) and others we know that Myos Hormos and Berenice were both linked by organized caravan-routes with Coptos on the Nile and so with the Egyptian markets. Between Berenice and Adulis, the small harbourless market-town of Ptolemais provided some sort of outlet for Meroe, the decayed capital of Nubia; but it was more important at this time to observe that behind Adulis lay the kingdom of the Axumites, in what is now Ethiopia or Abyssinia, established not long before by immigrants who had been squeezed out of southern Arabia by combined Arab and Parthian pressure. Now, in alliance with Rome, it became an entrepôt of African and Eastern trade, particularly as a focus for African ivory, and received a miscellany of imports which included gold and silver plate for the king and iron and muslin from India.

On the eastern and more barbarous shore of the Red Sea, there was a harbour and fort called Leukē Kōmē (White Town), whence there was a road to the Nabataean city of Petra. The interesting information is added that a Roman centurion was stationed there with an armed force to collect one-fourth of the merchandise imported. Further south and more important commercially was the market-town of Muza, situated not far from the narrow outlet of the Bab-el-mandeb. The region was under Arab rule (see p. 138), but Rome had established trading rights at the town, placating the king with gifts of 'horses and sumpter-mules, vessels of gold and polished silver, finely woven clothing and copper vessels'. The same king controlled the anchorage of Ocelis, actually within the straits, which according to Pliny's informant (*N.H.* vi, 104) was the most convenient port for those arriving from India. This information should perhaps be read in the light of the further statement of the *Periplus* in regard to Eudaemon Arabia (Aden). Eudaemon had 'convenient anchorages and watering-places sweeter and better than those of Ocelis', and, 'when the voyage was not yet made direct from India to Egypt, and when they did not dare to sail from Egypt to the ports across this ocean, all came together at this place. It received the cargoes from both countries, just as Alexandria now receives the things brought both from abroad and from Egypt'. Recently, however, Eudaemon had been destroyed in circumstances that are not now clear, though the removal of the entrepôt to Ocelis points suspiciously to the king of Muza as a party to the fact. Behind the episode emerges the significant circumstance that, whether in the Gulf of Aden or in the actual entry to the Red Sea, hereabouts was a traditional barrier where long-range traffic was withheld from its ultimate Red Sea markets and Arab middlemen took charge. The establishment of Roman privileges at Muza marks an attempt to reduce the costly impact of these middlemen, who presumably still secured their pickings even though (as the *Periplus* states) direct voyages were now undertaken between India and Egypt.

Along the incense-bearing shores of southern Arabia we need not follow our geographer in detail. Thinking back to the rich Roman wares from the undocumented regions of Free Germany, we may again note that the king of Sabratha in the Hadramaut received 'wrought gold and silver plate, also horses, images, and thin clothing of fine quality', either as propitiatory gifts or as selected imports. Further, we are told that an unattractive but convenient island, Dioscoride (the modern Socotra), off Cape Gardafui had become a trading-post manned by a few hardy agents – Arabs, Indians, and Greeks. Traders from western and southern India brought to this island 'rice and wheat and

Indian cloth, and a few female slaves', and took away in exchange ' a great quantity of tortoise-shell'. To the east along the Arabian coast, Moscha (near the modern Taka) was a speically privileged port of call much used in the Indian trade; 'ships returning from Damirica [South India] and Barygaza [Broach in Gujarat], if the season is late, winter there and trade with the king's officers, exchanging their cloth and wheat and sesame oil for frankincense'.

Thereafter our merchant turns northwards up the Persian Gulf, at the head of which was a treaty-port called Apologos, later known as Obollah, near Charax Spasini and the mouths of the Euphrates. His information in regard to this region is sketchy and perhaps second-hand, but at such brief times as the Parthian rulers were not at loggerheads with Rome the port must have been an important meeting-place of sea and land traffic. To it and to 'another market-town of Persia called Ommana', apparently on the Arabian shore of the Gulf, large vessels were sent from western India with cargoes of copper, sandalwood, teak, blackwood, and ebony, in return for local pearls ('inferior to those of India'), purple dye, local clothing, wine, dates, gold, and slaves.

Of all this Arabian trade, based primarily on the export of incense and secondarily on the transmission of goods to and from Egypt and the Orient, scarcely any material evidence of the Imperial period has yet been brought to light along its recorded routes. Little search has indeed been made for such evidence, though regret for this omission is tempered by the general clarity of the written record. No doubt the careful excavation of a site such as that of Adulis would amplify the story in rewarding fashion, and would in particular give a new precision to the Indian contribution. To that contribution the second half of the Greek 'handbook' is devoted (fig. 16).

Fig. 16

The *Periplus* first strikes the Indo-Pakistan sub-continent at the shallow, marshy delta of the river Indus, here transcribed as 'Sinthus'. The region was at the time occupied by Scythians under Parthian rule, presumably from the Parthian metropolis of Taxila in the Punjab. At the mouth of the Indus was the market-town of Barbáricum, and inland behind it was the Scythian capital of Minnagara.

The site of neither place is known with certainty to-day, though the guess that Hyderabad in Sind, at the head of the Indus delta, may represent alike the ancient Minnagara and the Patala of Alexander the Great is geographically reasonable. The imports and exports through Barbaricum form an interesting list. From the west came 'a great deal of thin clothing, and a little spurious; figured linens, topaz, coral, storax [an incense], frankincense, vessels of glass, silver and gold plate, and a little wine'. On the other hand, there were exported costus (a culinary spice and a perfume), bdellium (an arómatic gum), lycium (a dye and a medicine), nard (a medicinal oil and perfume), turquoise, lapis lazuli, Seric (central or eastern Asiatic) skins, muslin, silk yarn, and indigo. Several of these commodities, notably the silk yarn, skins, and stones, must have travelled long distances before they were shipped at the Indus delta. More will be said of this at a later stage.

From the Indus our merchant works his way down the west coast of India, noting especially Barygaza, the modern Broach, on the coast of Gujarat, predecessor of the later 'factory' of Surat on the same coast. The adjacent country, he observes, was particularly fertile, yielding wheat and rice, sesame oil, clarified butter (*ghee*), cotton and the Indian cloths made therefrom of the coarser sorts. In spite of its difficult seaward approaches the port was of the first importance in the India trade. From the wealthy cities of central India it was accessible by the arterial valleys of the Narbada and the Tapti, and routes of no great difficulty supplied it from Rajputana and the north. Incidentally, the *Periplus* mentions the interesting fact that 'ancient drachmas bearing inscriptions in Greek letters and the devices of those who reigned after Alexander' were still in circulation there, having drifted down from Bactria and north-western India as to-day they still drift (in original or in imitation) into the hands of the Bombay dealers.

Again, the imports and exports are worth noting. The former included 'wine, Italian preferred, also Laodicean and Arabian; copper, tin, and lead; coral and topaz; thin clothing and inferior sorts of all kinds; bright-coloured girdles a cubit wide; storax, sweet clover, glass, realgar [a medicinal gum], antimony, gold and silver coin, on which there is a profit when exchanged for the money of the country; and ointment'. In accordance with a diplomatic usage with which we are now familiar, 'for the king there are brought very costly vessels of silver, singing boys, beautiful maidens for the harem, fine wines, thin clothing of the finest weaves, and the choicest ointments'. The exports comprised spikenard (a Himalayan herb which produced a valued medicinal ointment), costus, bdellium, ivory, agate and carnelian, lycium, muslin of all kinds, silk cloth, mallow cloth (of coarse, purple-dyed cotton), yarn, long pepper and other things.

South of Barygaza, Kalliena (modern Kalyāna, near Bombay) had at one time been a port offering trading facilities, but in the time of the *Periplus* its use was being obstructed by the local ruler. South again, nine other places are mentioned, together with certain islands which harboured pirates. More important were Muziris and Nelcynda, the former of which may probably be identified with Cranganore in the Cochin backwaters; the latter was not far distant, but was situated in another Indian kingdom. These places were in 'Damirika', amended from the Limyrike of the text to conform with the Ravenna Geographer (Dimirica) and the Peutinger Table (Damirika), which shows the region in its Segment XII and marks, incidentally, a 'Templum Augusti' at Muziris. The Roman temple has not been found nor have small-scale excavations

at Cranganore revealed any evidences of Roman occupation hereabouts, but the area of potentiality is very
large and much further search is required.

The Cochin backwaters are to-day and have long been
the home of a remarkable assemblage of races and creeds:
communities of Jews, Syrians, Roman Catholics alongside
Hindus, each group with its characteristic meeting-places,
sometimes of considerable antiquity. The germ of this
cosmopolitanism doubtless goes back to the days of Imperial trade, and a Roman temple amongst the palms would
accord with the heterogeneous traditions of the scene. The
prime attraction to the western trader was the accessibility
of these sheltered waterways to the pepper which, then
as now, flourished in the hinterland of the moist Malabar
coast. Much could be and indeed has been written of pepper
and its bearing on the ways of man. To leave the *Periplus*
for a moment, Pliny (*N.H.* XII, 14) has an eloquent passage
from the Roman standpoint: 'It is quite surprising that the
use of pepper has come so much into fashion, seeing that,
in other substances which we use, it is sometimes their
sweetness and sometimes their appearance that has attracted
our notice; whereas, pepper has nothing in it that can plead
as a recommendation to either fruit or berry, its only
desirable quality being a certain pungency; and yet it is
for this that we import it all the way from India! Who
was the first to make trial of it as an article of food? And
who, I wonder, was the man that was not content to pre-
pare himself by hunger only for the satisfaction of a greedy
appetite?' From the Roman world the taste for pepper
spread to barbarian Europe; it will suffice to recall that
Alaric the Goth demanded 3,000 lb of it in his treaty with
the Romans in A.D. 408. And, to carry the story to a much
later date, in 1592 the pepper carried by a Spanish East
Indian carrack captured by Frobisher's ships off the Azores

was alone worth £102,000. In retrospect it is scarcely surprising that the filling of the Pepper Barns beside the Tiber was a primary function of Roman trade with the Orient.

In addition to pepper, the *Periplus* includes amongst the exports from the Malabar coast 'great quantities of fine pearls, ivory, silk cloth, spikenard from the Ganges, malabathrum [an equivalent of cinnamon] from the places in the interior, transparent stones of all kinds, diamonds and sapphires, and tortoiseshell. This is a fairly comprehensive list. The diamonds, if such they really were, probably came from central India; the pearls coastwise from the neighbourhood of Cape Comorin; the silk by sea from China. The popularity of the market was doubtless due in part to the fact that it could be reached from the Red Sea by a direct trans-oceanic route of which more will be said, with the added advantage that the perils of coastal piracy were thereby reduced to a minimum. The corresponding imports from the west were 'primarily a great quantity of coin; topaz; thin clothing, not much; figured linens, antimony, coral, crude glass, copper, tin, lead; wine, not much, but as much as at Barygaza; realgar and orpiment [a yellow sulphide of arsenic for making yellow paint, from the Persian Gulf]; and wheat enough for the sailors, for this is not dealt in by the merchants there'.

South of Muziris and Nelcynda the *Periplus* is more summary and confused, but the general sequence of place-names probably remains correct. After the Cape of Comari (Cape Comorin) we come to Colchi, famous for its pearl-fisheries, which were worked by condemned criminals; and thence, proceeding from south to north, we reach successively the market-towns of Camara, Podoukē and Sopatma. Of these, Camara is uncertain unless it be a variant of Ptolemy's *Khabēris emporion* at the mouth of the Khabēros or Kāverī (Cauvery) river, where the present

Tranquebar represents the former Kāvēripatnam or Kāv-erīppattinam. Podoukē may be equated with Pondicherry or Pudu-chchēre ('Newtown'), near which an Indo-Roman emporium has in fact been discovered (p. 173). With less evidence, Sopatma has been identified with the So-pattinam of Tamil literature, the modern Markanam, on the coast between Pondicherry and Madras.

Ceylon is referred to as 'the island Palaesimundu, called by the ancients Taprobane' but was clearly unknown to the writer, for a reason which will be suggested at a later stage. Meanwhile, we may follow the *Periplus* up the east coast of India, past Masalia, which may be the port of Masuli-patam, where 'a great quantity of muslin is made', to the mouth of the Ganges, 'and near it the very last land to-wards the east, Chrysē' or Golden, presumably the Malay peninsula, known to Ptolemy as the Aurea Chersonesus. On the Ganges was a market-town of the same name, through which were brought malabathrum, spikenard and pearls, and muslins of the finest sorts; and gold-mines and gold coinage (presumably from the Kushāna empire further west) are mentioned.

North of Chrysē lay China, the land called This, 'diffi-cult of access', whence 'raw silk and silk yarn and silk cloth are brought on foot through Bactria to Barygaza, and are also exported to Damirica [South India] by way of the river Ganges'. The *Periplus* ends with a picturesque description of the mongoloid traders who come together 'every year on the borders of the land of This, a tribe of men with short bodies and broad flat faces, and by nature peaceable. . . . They come with their wives and children, carrying great packs and plaited baskets of what looks like green grape-leaves.' One would like to see in this an early reference to tea, but the commodity was in fact probably malabathrum from the Himalaya.

So much for the *Periplus*. Its information is elaborated
by other classical writers, but stands first for actuality.
Ptolemy, however, compiling his geography about A.D.
150 from a variety of sources including, as he tells us, 'those
who have sailed from us to those places and have for a long
time frequented them', had nearly a century's further
general knowledge behind him and supplements the story.
In particular, as we shall see, he knew significantly more
about Ceylon than did his predecessor, and his information
about the interior of India, however distorted, was not
inconsiderable. Along the coast he largely duplicates but
also extends the earlier list, and it may be that on one
important matter of administration he combines with
Strabo, Pliny, and above all the *Periplus* to throw a little
light.

Round the coast of India and Ceylon, from the Indus to
the Ganges, sixteen of the coastal towns are singled out by
him as *emporia* (e.g. *Muziris emporion*, *Pōdoukē emporion*),
which were presumably trading-ports in some special sense.
The suggestion is that in each maritime district there was,
amongst other places, one which was pre-eminently *the*
commercial port, with rights or privileges which it is not
Ptolemy's business to define. This recalls the use of the
phrase *nomimon emporion* ('lawful market') by the *Periplus*
in respect of Adulis, Muza, and Apologos, or of *enthesmon
emporion* ('privileged market') in respect of Kalliena, near
Bombay. In these instances there is a clear indication of
special legal provision for trading; and some variant of
this provision is presumably implied in the word *apodedeig-
menos* ('designated'), which the same authority attaches
to Myos Hormos on the Red Sea and Moscha on the
Arabian coast, though the word may rather indicate the
canalization of certain types of traffic through these two
places. Two passages in the *Periplus* seem to have a bearing

on the matter: at Kalliena a new raja had cancelled or at least obstructed rights conferred on traders by a predecessor, to the extent of arresting Greek ships on arrival; and at Leukē Kōmē, an emporium 'for small vessels' on the eastern side of the Red Sea, there was, as we have seen, actually a military post under a centurion to ensure that the Arabs respected trading rights and to collect a duty of twenty-five per cent on imports. It is evident, by and large, that the privileges of Western traders were differently safeguarded in the various foreign ports; that in one place (probably exceptional) Roman authority, even a Roman Customs levy, might be guaranteed by a Roman garrison, and that in another the trafficking was subject to the good will of a local ruler, who might be encouraged by diplomatic gifts (pp. 142, 143) to grant and observe concessions, but at long range retained the power to discontinue them. It is likely enough that in the *emporia* were normally posted permanent agencies of the Graeco-Roman traders, organized on lines not unlike those of the Portuguese, Dutch, Danish, French, or British 'factories' in the India trade of a much later date. Indeed, it is fair to envisage Indo-European commerce of the first century A.D. pretty closely in terms of that of the seventeenth century; that is, it was based on mutual advantage endorsed by Western prestige and sufficiently regulated to ensure continuity.

CHAPTER TEN

THE MONSOON

BOTH the *Periplus* and Pliny have something of interest to say about the systems of navigation upon which the Imperial commerce with India was based. When he reaches the Indus delta, the author of the *Periplus* records that 'sailors set out thither with the Indian Etesian winds, about the month of July, that is Epiphi: it is more dangerous then,[1] but through these winds the voyage is more direct and sooner completed'. The Etesian winds, as Strabo tells us, brought the summer rains to India, and were in fact the south-western monsoon which begins regularly at the end of June and lasts until September. By keeping it on the quarter, the sailors from the ports near the mouth of the Red Sea were able to steer a tolerably straight course across the approaches to the Persian Gulf, 'quite away from the land', to the Indus and Barygaza. Similarly, those making for Damirica or South India sailed direct a little south of east across the Arabian Sea, throwing the ship's head considerably off the wind and in favourable circumstances making the voyage to Muziris, as Pliny tells us, in forty days. 'Hippalus', adds the *Periplus*, 'was the pilot who, by observing the location of the ports and the condition of the sea, first discovered how to lay his course straight across the ocean.'

Hippalus is one of the great names in the history of navigation. Without his discovery, or at least his popularization of the monsoon as a dependable aid to deep-sea voyaging, regular trade with India would have been impossible. The long coastwise journey was alike excessively tedious, and fraught with recurrent danger from piracy.

1. The principal danger arose (and arises) from following seas, liable to overtake and swamp small, slow craft.

The history of the India trade is therefore very incomplete without some agreement as to the date of Hippalus, and agreement has not hitherto been reached in the matter. Our only other historical authority is Pliny, whose account must be summarized and considered (*N.H.* VI, 26). Pliny distinguishes four stages in the development of navigation between the Red Sea and India. At first there was only the long coastal route taken by the fleet of Alexander; small vessels sailed from Aden, along the shores of southern Arabia and Makran, and made the Indus and the west coast of the sub-continent. 'In later times it has been thought that the safest line is to start from Ras Fartak in Arabia with a west wind, the local name for which is the Hippalus, and make for Patale [at the mouth of the Indus], the distance being reckoned as 1,332 miles. The following generation [i.e. the third stage of our series] considered it a shorter and safer route to start from the same cape and steer for the Indian harbour of Sigerus [probably south of Bombay], and for a long time this was the course followed, until a merchant discovered a shorter route [our fourth stage], and the desire for gain brought India nearer; indeed the voyage is made every year, with companies of archers on board, because the seas are very greatly infested by pirates.'

It will be observed that neither the *Periplus* nor Pliny suggests a date for Hippalus. Moreover, whilst the *Periplus* associates Hippalus vaguely with the use of the monsoon in general, Pliny attaches his name only to the second of his four stages – namely, the straight voyage from the Arabian coast to the Indus. Both writers imply that Hippalus was a historical, not a contemporary, figure; Pliny indeed separates him by an 'age' or 'generation' from the third stage, which was in turn a 'long time' before the fourth stage. It is clear that Hippalus lived some very considerable time before the third quarter of the first century A.D. to which the composition of the *Periplus* and the *Natural History* may both be assigned.

It is therefore historically unlikely that Pliny's second stage, specifically that of Hippalus, was as late as A.D. 40–1, the date to which E. H. Warmington has attributed it in his excellent book on *The Commerce between the Roman Empire and India*. Other writers, notably W. W. Tarn in *The Greeks in Bactria and India*, have put the Hippalus stage as early as 80 B.C. or even earlier. Without reconsideration of these views, two pieces of evidence which have emerged more recently may be brought to bear upon the problem. The first seems to relate to Pliny's story of the freedman of one Annius Plocamus who in the reign of Claudius (so Pliny implies) farmed the collection of Red Sea taxes. The freedman, while sailing round Arabia, was carried out of his course by northern gales which swept him in a fortnight (*sic*) from the coast of Persia to that of Ceylon. As Warmington remarks: 'Here we have a man who did not know the use of the monsoon winds in order to reach Ceylon.' If from this we take the further, somewhat reckless step of inferring that during a part of the reign of Claudius the use of the monsoon had not yet been adequately advertised, then the late dating of Hippalus might appear to receive some support. Latterly, however, Dr David Meredith, in studying the ancient inscriptions of the Eastern Desert of Egypt, has drawn attention to an extremely interesting rock inscription, a graffito duplicated in Latin and Greek, in a sheltered spot beside the old road from Coptos to Berenice, at a distance of about sixty-eight miles from Coptos.[1] The Latin version reads:

LYSA P. ANNI PLOCAMI VENI ANNO XXXV
III. NON IVL. . . .

1. *Journ. of Roman Studies*, XLIII (1953), 38.

The meaning is clear enough: the graffito is a casual record of one Lysas, a slave of Publius Annius Plocamus, who came that way and presumably sheltered from the midday sun in the thirty-fifth year of the Emperor's reign (*Kaisaros* is added in the Greek version). This Emperor can only have been Augustus, and the date is therefore July 5th, A.D. 6. Identity of this Annius Plocamus with Pliny's is not proved and that of the two freedmen is not of course suggested, but the coincidence of the name in so appropriate a geographical setting amounts to near-proof in respect of Plocamus, and it would be wise to consider the date of his errant freedman in Ceylon as likely to have been appreciably earlier than the reign of Claudius.

Be that as it may, of far greater account is the discovery of an Indo-Roman trading-station at Arikamedu, the native name of a waterside tract within a few hundred yards of the Bay of Bengal two miles south of Pondicherry (p. 173), which almost certainly equates etymologically with the 'Podoukē' of the *Periplus* and the 'Pōdoukē emporion' of Ptolemy. The small area excavated here in 1945 yielded thirty-one sherds of Italic (Arretine) ware, and a score or more of additional fragments have been found before and since that year. Now, Arretine ware of the kinds now in question seems to have been made first about 30 B.C.; more certainly, it went out of manufacture about A.D. 45, and its extensive export to the far side of India may be pivoted on a central date within the bracket, i.e. within the first two decades of the first century A.D. But the postulation of a series of trading-posts of this kind – for Pōdoukē was, as we have seen, only one of a series – upon the east coast of India carries with it the postulation of regular trade with the West, and this in turn implies monsoon traffic. The 'Hippalus' may now be assumed therefore to have been in full and undisguised use at the end of the reign of Augustus (died A.D. 14); and incidentally the assumption gives a new actuality to the statement of Strabo, writing under Augustus, that from the Egyptian port of Myos Hormos alone 120 ships left for the East every year.

Whether the 'Hippalus' was known, and if so to whom, before the latter years of Augustus is another matter. It may well have been a trade secret of the Arab middlemen or their Indian agents long before it became familiar to the shipping companies of Rome and Alexandria. The apparent fact that an Augustan tax-collector's freedman had not heard of it does not imply a corresponding ignorance on the part of the professional sea-carriers of Muza or Barygaza. At least as early as the second century B.C. Indians occasionally found their way to Egypt, and a Greek now and then to India; and in the earlier half of the first century B.C. pepper was already reaching the Mediterranean in some quantity, probably via Syria.[1] None of these various circumstances proves or disproves awareness of the 'Hippalus' by Greeks, Indians, or Arabs before the reign of Augustus. Nevertheless it cannot be without significance that the first flood of Western coinage to reach India was Augustan; with it were a few Republican *denarii*, mostly worn, but Ptolemaic issues are unknown there, or practically so, and Strabo (17. 1. 13) observes that prior to his time 'not so many as twenty vessels would dare to traverse the Arabian Gulf far enough to get a peep outside the straits'. The one certain point, be it insisted, is that the regularization and development of the India trade in the principate of Augustus was to a large extent rendered possible, if not by Hippalus himself, at least by the fact that his discovery and its further implications were now for the first time common knowledge.

1. W. W. Tarn, *The Greeks in Bactria and India* (Cambridge, 1951), pp. 370-1.

CHAPTER ELEVEN

FROM THE INDIAN STANDPOINT

DEVOID though they be of the historical framework of the classical records, Indian literature and epigraphy contain numerous references to these or other contacts with the West. As early as the middle of the third century B.C. the Buddhist emperor Ašoka could write in two of the famous edicts which he had graven on rocks and pillars up and down India that he was, potentially at least, in diplomatic relations with the rulers of the eastern Mediterranean – Antiochos Theos, king of Syria and Western Asia; Ptolemy Philadelphos, king of Egypt; Magas, king of Cyrene; Antigonos Gonatas, king of Macedonia; and perhaps Alexander, king of Epirus. This is a formidable list. Ašoka cites it in connexion with his proselytizing activities amongst his 'neighbours', but, even in the absence of archaeological evidence, it would not be unfair to suspect that this high-level neighbourliness had a material basis in the form of trade, though material evidence for this is lacking. A century later, Menander, most brilliant of the Greek kings of north-western India, became (then or subsequently) the hero of a didactic historical romance, *The Questions of Milinda*, which refers incidentally to maritime trade with 'Vanga [Bengal], or Takkola, or China, or Sovira, or Surat [on the Gujarat coast], or Alexandria, or the Coromandel Coast, or Further India'.[1] Where or when the *Questions* were first written down is uncertain,[2] but

---

1. T. W. Rhys Davids, *The Questions of Milinda* (Sacred Books of the East Series, Oxford, 1890), II, 269. See also W. W. Tarn, *The Greeks in Bactria and India* (1951), pp. 414ff.

2. For discussion, see Tarn, pp. 416ff.

indications point to a date for the oldest surviving version at or a little after the beginning of the Christian era, so that the reference may reflect in part the organized commerce of Augustus rather than the actual circumstances of Menander's own time. It at least presents India as the focus of a far-flung traffic, which is itself a little suggestive of the later period.

In the story Menander (or Milinda) has a council of 500 'Yonakas'. The number was doubtless exaggerated, but the general circumstance is not unlikely. The word 'Yonaka' is apparently a Hellenistic variant of the more usual term 'Yavana', and is equivalent to 'Ionian', i.e. Greek. The word reappears in a Prakrit inscription at Nasik near Bombay in a Buddhist cave which has commonly been dated to the first century B.C., but may be half a century later. Here also and at similar caves at Junnar and Karli in the same region are eight other inscriptions recording dedications by donors who describe themselves as Yavanas. The names of these donors are Indian, and the description of them as 'Greek' presumably implies that they or their forebears had come from cities in the former Indo-Greek kingdom further north; the Yonaka indeed tells us that he was 'Indragnitta, son of Dhammadeva, a Yonaka of Demetrias', a Greek foundation in Sind. In the present context the significance of these circumstances is that they presume a certain preparedness on the part of wealthy Indian merchants of the first centuries B.C.-A.D. for further contact with the western world.

Apart from this apparent use of 'Yavana' and 'Yonaka' in a secondary sense, the Yavanas of Indian literature are normally Westerners in the fullest meaning of the term. The Tamil poems of the so-called 'Sangam' age of the earlier centuries A.D. contain repeated references to them.[1] Thus, 'agitating the white foam of the Periyaru, the beautifully built ships of the Yavanas came with gold and returned with pepper, and Muziris resounded with the noise'. In another poem a Pāndya (South Indian) prince is exhorted to drink the cool and fragrant wines brought by the Yavanas in their vessels. The epic known as *The Lay of the Anklet* ('Śilappadikāram') describes vividly the quarter of the city of Puhār or Kāvēripattinam at the mouth of the Kāvēri river – almost certainly Ptolemy's *Khabēris emporion* 'The sun shone over the open terraces, over the warehouses near the harbour and over the turrets with windows like the eyes of deer. In different places of Puhār the onlooker's attention was caught by the sight of the abodes of Yavanas, whose prosperity never waned. At the harbour were to be seen sailors from many lands, but to all appearances they lived as one community . . .' And Tamil rajas employed bodyguards of western mercenaries, 'the valiant-eyed Yavanas whose bodies were strong and of terrible aspect' and who, equipped with 'murderous swords', were excellent guardians of the gates of the fort-walls'. In this capacity they are said to have been employed at Madura. Yavana craftsmen were also sought after in southern India, especially for the manufacture of siege-engines, whilst in the north, as a third-century legend has it, St Thomas was brought to the court of king Gondopharnes (*c.* A.D. 19-45) at Taxila for his skill as a builder of 'pillars, temples, and courthouses for kings'. In one way and another, the Yavana *in partibus* enjoyed a considerable prestige whether as trader or as settler.

That this various interchange was not unsought by the

1. See V. Kanakasabhai, *The Tamils Eighteen Hundred Years Ago* (Madras and Bangalore, 1904); P. T. Srinivas Iyengar, *History of the Tamils from the Earliest Times to* 600 *A.D.* (Madras, 1929); *The Śilappadikāram*, trans. V. R. Ramachandra Dikshitar (Oxford, 1939).

Indians themselves is clear enough, alike by the presence of Indian sailors and agents along the coasts of Arabia and Africa, as indicated by the *Periplus*, and by the repeated arrival of Indian missions at the court of the Roman emperor. Augustus declares in his monumental record at Ankara that these missions came to him 'frequently'; and, though it is not always easy to distinguish the various occasions from one another, there is more or less specific evidence for at least four of them during his principate. Thus at Antioch an Indian embassy to Augustus was seen by Nicolaus of Damascus and subsequently noted by Strabo (15. 1. 73), who tells us that it came from 'Porus', a king of kings probably in the Punjab, where the name or title was traditional. Owing to the hardships of the long journey, only three of the delegates had survived, but they brought with them a letter written in Greek on parchment together with gifts, including a man born without arms, snakes, a large river-turtle, a partridge 'bigger than a vulture', and a sophist from Bargosa or Barygaza who in fanatical fervour burned himself at Athens and was commemorated there by 'the Indian's tomb' (Plutarch, *Alexander*, LXIX). The Greek letter affirmed that Porus was 'anxious to be a friend to Caesar, and was ready, not only to allow him a passage through his country wherever he wished to go, but also to co-operate with him in anything that was honourable' – a sentiment which suggests the effusive adumbration of a trade agreement. Strabo (15. 1. 4) also mentions an embassy to Augustus from a king 'Pandion', who probably ruled over Pandya, the southernmost kingdom of India. Embassies were apparently received by Augustus in Spain in 26 or 25 B.C. and at Samos in 21 B.C.,[1] and Horace refers to one or other of these missions in his *Carmen Saeculare*. Vaguer references (for

1. For these and other embassies, see Warmington, pp. 35ff.

F

example, by the second-century 'Annaeus Florus') tell us
of Indian embassies bringing elephants, precious stones, and
pearls to Augustus; and we are left in no doubt that in his
time there was a new rapprochement between East and
West unparalleled since the time of Alexander.

Later emperors continued to receive embassies from the
sub-continent. To Claudius, as Pliny tells us (*N.H.* VI, 84),
came four envoys from the king of Ceylon, 'banished by
nature beyond the confines of the world' and previously –
as is clear enough from Pliny's account – unfamiliar with
the West. The mission is said to have originated from the
curiosity aroused there by the castaway freedman of
Plocamus referred to above (p. 155). It obviously did not
understate the wealth of the island; certainly Roman trade
was shortly afterwards extended to it, and Ptolemy in the
following century was able for the first time to give an
adequate description of it. Again, in A.D. 107 amongst the
embassies received by Trajan was one from India (Dio,
LXVIII, 15); and we are reminded that in his last years, his
thoughts full of Alexander, the old emperor stood on the
shores of the Persian Gulf and, seeing a ship sailing away to
India, exclaimed: 'Above all things would I have passed
over to India, were I still young.' Throughout the second
and early third century Indian envoys continued to arrive
from time to time. Hadrian received envoys from the
'Bactrian kings', who are probably relevant to a part of our
story; and to Antoninus Pius came ambassadors from the
'Indians, Bactrians, and Hyrcanians'. Even later, when the
Eastern trade was under a cloud, Elagabalus, Aurelian, and
Constantine the Great are recorded nevertheless to have
received missions.[1] The lively interest of India in the

1. See M. P. Charlesworth in *Studies in Roman Economic and
Social History*, ed. by P. R. Coleman-Norton (Princeton Univ.
Press, 1951), p. 140.

Yavanas and their markets needs no further advertisement.

Yet, were it not for the impressive witness of history, the magnitude of this trade would certainly not have been guessed. Material relics of it in the West are few, very few, for the good and obvious reason that most of them were of an impermanent kind. Best of the rare survivors is the well-known ivory statuette of Lakshmi, the Indian goddess of good luck and prosperity, found at Pompeii and therefore brought there prior to A.D. 79 (pl. 15).[1] It is a charming minor work of Indian art of a sort which is commonly, though not compellingly, associated with the Kushāna capital of Mathurā (Muttra), south of Delhi, and may well have found its way out of India through Barygaza. A case, too, has been stated more than once for the derivation of the squatting posture of the Gaulish god Cernunnos from India, and astonishingly Oriental the posture sometimes is. But alternative explanations are possible and more likely.[2] The squatting or 'Buddhistic' attitude is indeed a recognized feature of Ligurian sculpture as early as the third or second century B.C. (for example, at Roquepertuse and Entremont in the neighbourhood of Aix-en-Provence), and is presumably a native element in this remarkable Graeco-Gallic amalgam.[3]

1. See A. Maiuri, 'Statuetta eburnea di arte indiana a Pompei', in *Le Arti* (Florence), 1938–9, pp. 111–15.

2. For a documented review, see P. F. Bober, 'Cernunnos: Origin and Transformation of a Celtic Deity', *American Journ. of Archaeology*, LV (1951), 13ff.

3. See F. Benoît in *Gallia* V (Paris, 1947), 81–97; and Benoît, *L'Art primitif méditerranéen de la Vallée du Rhône: la Sculpture* (Paris, 1954).

CHAPTER TWELVE

SOUTH INDIA

THE *Periplus* indicates clearly enough that the traffic with India was basically of two kinds. There were goods which were produced by the sub-continent itself, and there were others which reached the Indian markets from further afield, particularly from central Asia and China. Trade of the former category may usefully be termed 'terminal trade'; that of the latter was 'transit trade'. Although at certain ports, such as Barygaza, the two groups of commodities would converge, they were essentially separate and may be separately considered.

The trade of central and southern India was mainly terminal trade. The spices, muslins, pearls, and jewel-stones which constituted the bulk of it came principally from those regions. On the showing of the *Periplus*, there may be added a modicum of transit trade, chiefly in the form of silk which, diverted by Parthian hostility from the more direct continental routes, sometimes found its way deviously from China via the east coast of India to the ports on the Malabar coast and so joined up with the direct monsoon route to the West. We are reminded that, centuries later, on this same cosmopolitan coast a colony of Chinese merchants and craftsmen established themselves and adequately prospered at Quilon. But in Roman times it may be suspected that the China trade normally found its way through more northerly ports in a manner to be discussed presently.

The importance of the South Indian trade with the West in the first century A.D. has long been underlined by the impressively abundant Roman coinage which has come to light fortuitously in the peninsula since 1775 (fig. 17). Of

Fig. 17. Distribution of Roman Coins in India

sixty-eight finds which (excluding those from Ceylon) are
known from the whole sub-continent – India and Pakistan together – no fewer than fifty-seven come from south
of the Vindhyas; and, with the exception of a stray

denarius of Tiberius at Taxila in the Punjab, *all* first-century
Roman coins not associated with later issues have been
found in the south. More precisely, twenty-nine finds,
distributed through Madras province and the states of
Hyderabad, Mysore, Cochin, Pudukottai, and Travancore,
comprise *aurei* or *denarii* ranging from Augustus to Trajan
(pl. 18). This mass of coinage demands analysis.

The first noteworthy point is that, of the twenty-nine
first-century finds, at least twenty are known to have constituted hoards, ranging individually from four or five coins
to 'some hundreds, if not thousands'. In the circumstances
it is reasonable to suspect that some of the ill-recorded
strays likewise represent hoards.

Secondly, these first-century coins are invariably of gold
or silver. There is no authenticated discovery of a Roman
'brass' coin of the first or second century in India.

Thirdly, coins of Augustus and Tiberius predominate.
After Nero they dwindle markedly.

Fourthly, the gold coins are liable to be either pierced
for suspension or mutilated by a cut across the obverse.
Only one of the very numerous Roman silver coins is
known to have been similarly mutilated.

Fifthly, there is a notable grouping of early coin-finds
across southern India from the western to the eastern coasts.

Of these five points, the first is readily explained in
relation to the second. The significance of hoards in general
has often been discussed, and they are commonly regarded
as savings lost, or rather not recovered, during a period of
disturbance. But it would be easy to overstress this aspect
of the matter, and, whatever the accidents of their final
deposition, it may be suggested that the preponderance of
early Roman hoards in South India first and foremost
represents an essentially economic factor. The great quantity of gold and silver coins imported by first-century

Roman trade into India is noted or implied by more than one classical writer. The *Periplus* mentions it in relation to Barygaza and as first amongst the imports carried by Western merchants to the Malabar ports; Pliny (VI, 101) remarks that 'in no year does India absorb less than fifty million sesterces', which presumably represented actual cash rather than the estimated value of wares; Tiberius may be thought to have had this extravagant efflux specially in mind when he complained to the Roman senate of the reckless exportation of money 'to foreign nations and even to the enemies of Rome' in exchange for gew-gaws (Tacitus, *Ann.* II, 53). But how was all this currency fitted into the alien economies of recipients far beyond the boundaries of the Roman Empire?

The clear answer is that, for the most part, it was employed not as currency but as bullion. In the whole of peninsular India there was no native currency of gold or silver to which the Roman coinage could be approximated. Pausanias (III, 12, 24) in the second century observed that the Indians exchanged their wares with those of the Greeks without understanding the use of money. The potin or lead coinage struck by the Andhra empire of central India in the first two centuries A.D. is a partial exception to this rule; and half a dozen scattered *denarii* of Augustus and Tiberius found over a period of years in a restricted area of an Andhra town at Chandravalli, near Chitaldrug in northern Mysore, if they do not represent a hoard broken anciently, may here have circulated in some ratio to the native base-metal issues. Outside the Andhra zone, however, this possibility does not arise. For the most part, the imported coins can only have been used as bullion, to be weighed out in exchange for goods as silver ornaments or scraps may be weighed out in an Indian bazaar to-day. Their normal occurrence in 'hoards' is a natural corollary.

Indeed, the term 'hoard' is in this context largely a mi
nomer; the so-called hoard being doubtless a unit
stamped silver or gold to a total weight agreed for som
specific purchase, or at least the bulk reserve from whic
such units could be detached. Monetary circulation in th
ordinary sense was not in question. The fact that th
precious metal was already subdivided into known an
stamped sub-units (coins) would nevertheless facilitate th
trader's accounting and at the same time carry prestig
with the customer. Pliny (VI, 85) tells a relevant story of th
admiration expressed by the king of Ceylon for Roma
honesty, on the ground that among the money found on
Roman castaway (Plocamus's famous freedman) the *denar*
were all equal in weight, although the various figures c
them showed that they had been coined by several emperor

This respect for Roman integrity was evidently shake
in India, as in Free Germany (p. 85), by Nero's debasemer
of his silver coinage in A.D. 63. The third of our poin
above needs no additional explanation. Just as in Free Ger
many the older pre-Neronic issues in pure silver wer
sought in preference to the alloyed issues subsequent to th
year 63, so in India silver issues later than Nero hardl
occur, whilst several hoards end with his reign or that c
his predecessor. And to this shaken confidence on th
Indian side in the bullion value of the newer *denarii* ma
be added export restrictions at source, arising from th
expressed anxiety of the Roman treasury at the enormou
outflow. That the India trade continued or even increase
after the time of Nero is clear from Ptolemy and from th
recent archaeological evidence of Arikamedu, which wi
be considered below. But it continued mainly in manu
factured goods and raw materials with only a modest re
inforcement from Roman gold and (much later) base meta

This brings us to our fourth point, the mutilation of th

gold coinage (two examples in pl. 18). The facts are as follows. Apart from occasional coins pierced for use as ornaments or charms, in at least six of the hoards the gold coins have, wholly or mostly, been defaced by an incision across the imperial head; and, since no other feature of the design, even when representation of the human figure is involved, has been singled out for this treatment, the purpose of the defacement was definitely not iconoclasm, but the cancellation of the piece as a coin-issue. The defaced coins cover a wide range of time, including issues of Claudius, Nero, Vespasian, Hadrian and, apparently in one case, Constantine.

For this mutilation there is no need to question the explanation long ago put forward by Sir George Hill that 'the incisions were made in India, in order to put the coins out of circulation'.[1] But an interesting fact may be added. Except in one *stūpa*-deposit, which as a votive offering may be regarded as a law unto itself, none of this Roman gold, whether mutilated or not, is found within the probable limits of the late first- and second-century Kūshāna empire, which included the whole of north-western India and the west-coast trading-ports of the Indus delta, Gujarat and Bombay. *Within* that empire was at this time struck the only native gold coinage of the period in India, and it was struck significantly to the Roman standard. In other words, it was in unconcealed competition with the Roman coinage and the suggestion has even been made that it consisted, at any rate in part, of re-struck Roman *aurei*. The implication is that all Roman gold which could be recovered was absorbed by the Kushāna empire and thus regulated or reminted; and the all-powerful Kushāns saw to it that such Roman gold as was admitted to their border states was

1. *Num. Chron.*, 3rd Series, XVIII (1898), 320; modified, *ib.* XIX (1899), 82.

removed by mutilation from possible rivalry as currency and relegated to use as bullion or ornament. The fact that most of this Roman gold is of first-century date, whereas the Kushāna empire reached its prime in the second century, is readily explained by Roman export restrictions from the latter part of the first century onwards and the consequence that little more than gold surviving in trade from the previous period was now in use.

The fact that a minority of the Roman gold was not mutilated implies, on this showing, merely the unequal reach of Kushāna interference or a measure of administrative laxity that requires no explanation in the East. In regard to imported silver, the question did not arise. As already remarked, no silver coinage comparable with the imported *denarii* existed in India in the first or second century A.D.; even the Kushāns issued none, with a single exception of Kadphises II in the British Museum and four coins, also unique, probably of his predecessor Kujūla Kadphises from Taxila.[1] Thus, unless very doubtfully in the Andhra kingdom, there was little risk of the intrusion of the *denarius* as currency since the country, including the Kushāna empire, was as a whole economically unprepared for it.

We may now turn to our fifth point, geographical distribution. Be it repeated that a large proportion of the Roman coins from India has been found in the peninsula, to the south of the Vindhyas and even to the south of the main Deccan plateau. Within this vast area, the district of Coimbatore and its borders, some 250 miles south-west of Madras, have produced more than the whole of the rest of the sub-continent put together. From the Coimbatore district alone there are at least eleven first-century hoards, running in the aggregate to many hundreds of gold and silver coins. As in all such cases, the first step is to refer to the map.

1. J. Marshall, *Taxila* (Cambridge, 1951), I, 68.

The district of Coimbatore is approached up two major
river-valleys, that of the Cauvery from the east coast and
that of the Ponnani from the west. It lies at the point where
the Eastern Ghats, swinging westwards, merge into the
Western Ghats and conspire with them to leave a trans-
verse gap, about twenty miles wide and only 1,000 feet high,

Fig. 18

between east and west. To-day through this, the Ponnani or
Pālghāt or Coimbatore gap, the railway from Madras and
the Carnatic plain penetrates to Calicut and Cochin; and
the traditional use of this route is indicated by the legend
which lands St Thomas on the Malabar coast near Cranganore and takes him thence overland to the Madras
coast.[1] Along this same route crowd the coins now in
question (fig. 18). Along it at first, we cannot doubt, came
the ancient traffic from Muziris (Cranganore) and Nelcynda

1. Warmington, p. 83.

to *Pōdoukē emporion* and *Khabēris emporion* (Arikamedu and Tranquebar) on the opposite coasts, evading the dangerous voyage round Cape Comorin. The avoidance of circumpeninsular navigation was a habit of ancient travelling. The little Cornish peninsula and the Jutland peninsula were thus short-circuited at one time or another. So too was peninsular India. Strabo in the time of Augustus wrote (15. 1. 4) that in his day only stray individuals had sailed round India to the Ganges and that they were 'of no use as regards the history of the places they had seen'. Pliny, as already related, had no recent knowledge of Ceylon until the embassy from the king of the island came to Rome with scrappy information in the time of Claudius. The *Periplus* becomes noticeably vague when, southbound, it leaves Nelcynda on the Malabar coast. Indeed Ptolemy, in the middle of the second century A.D., is our first circumstantial authority for those parts, and it has been observed that, in writing of Ceylon, he appears to have been making a display of information that was largely new to his reader. It is a fair inference that the Roman agencies established in the east coast ports under Augustus and Tiberius were, so far as the Westerners were concerned, the termini of transpeninsular routes, and that only towards the end of the first century were the western and eastern ports linked also by regular circumpeninsular traffic. Consistently with this, no coins earlier than Nero and Vespasian are recorded from Ceylon.

If there are, then, clear geographical reasons for the short-circuiting of wealth and traffic through Coimbatore, it is fair to ask why did so appreciable a proportion of it come to rest there? The question cannot at present be answered. According to an unconfirmed but plausible Tamil tradition, the three ancient kingdoms of South India – Chola, Chera, and Pandya – met in the Coimbatore district, and such a convergence of frontiers, providing alternative escapes, is at all times a favourite focus of brigandage. The hiding and loss of some part of this bullion would fit easily enough into that picture. Other hoards may represent the forgotten treasury of local prospectors and miners concerned with the famous beryl mines of the district, or of the owners of the pepper estates which doubtless spread, as to-day, on and below the 3,000 feet contour in the fringes of the district. There is reason to suppose that search would reveal ample evidence of occupation hereabouts, and excavation is now the necessary preliminary to further knowledge. Only at the eastern end of the zone, on the Coromandel Coast, has serious digging so far been attempted, and here the results have been immediate and dramatic.

Two miles south of Pondicherry, the former capital of French India, a former outlet of the Gingee river forms a lagoon locked to-day by a sand-bar from the Bay of Bengal, from which it is further sheltered by dunes and coconut palms. A part of the eastern bank of the lagoon stands some twenty feet above the water and from the scarp project the jagged ends of successive brick buildings to which the mound owes its being (pls. 16, 17, A and B, and 19, A and B). To the villagers the site is known as Arikamedu; French archaeologists have preferred to name it from a neighbouring village, Virampatnam. The fragments of walling were noted as long ago as the eighteenth century, but it was in 1937 that the site first attracted archaeological attention.

In that year village children brought to a local French antiquary a number of relics which they had picked up on the surface, amongst them a gem (now lost) which is reported to have borne an intaglio portrait of Augustus. Subsequently French and Indian investigators carried out some useful if summary digging on the site, and amongst the resultant finds the present writer in 1944 detected sherds of Italian red-glazed 'Arretine' ware and of amphorae from the Mediterranean, together with a fragment of a Roman lamp and a second Graeco-Roman gem, an untrimmed crystal intaglio representing a cupid and a bird. The Arretine ware was of the early first century A.D. In 1945 a systematic excavation was carried out for three months by the Archaeological Survey of India under the writer's direction, and the work was resumed for the French Government by Mr J. M. Casal in 1947–8.[1] The accumulated material of Western origin supplements with important detail the general historical and numismatic evidence given above, whilst, from the Indian standpoint, it has for the first time provided a firm and widely applicable datum for the associated native culture. The excavations have thus combined in a happy manner the interests alike of Western and of Indian archaeology.

Much of the town has been removed by the river, and its former landward extent is unknown, but the excavations of man and nature have identified a nucleus over 400 yards from north to south along the bank. Under the southern part of this area have been found the traces of a village associated with smooth black-and-brown pottery of the distinctive kind used by the builders of megalithic tombs in South India between *c.* 200 B.C. and A.D. 50. This village, like its modern equivalents in the neighbourhood, doubtless consisted of simple fisher-folk who caught the gullible fish of the region from the shore or from small outriggers, gathered the fruits and juices of the palms, cultivated rice-patches, and lived in a leisurely and unenter-

1. For the 1945 and earlier work, see *Ancient India*, No. 2 (Delhi, 1946), pp. 17ff.; for the 1947–8 work, see J. M. Casal, *Fouilles de Virampatnam-Arikamedu* (Paris, Imprimerie Nationale, 1949); also *Aspects of Archaeology* (*Essays to O. G. S. Crawford*) (London, 1951), pp. 354ff.; and *Germania* 1952, p. 389.

prising fashion just above subsistence level. To it suddenly, from unthought-of lands 5,000 miles away, came strange wines, table-wares far beyond the local skill, lamps of a strange sort, glass, cut gems. Traders arrived across-country from the west coast to meet the large Indian east coast ships of which the *Periplus* tells us, laden with gemstones from Ceylon, pearls from Kolchoi (Colchi), or spices and silks from the Ganges. A small foreign quarter like that of Puhār (p. 158) came into being, and finally the village was replaced by a brick-built town, spreading northwards to the sea. There is no reasonable doubt that this *new town* was the *Pōdoukē* of the *Periplus*, and *Pōdoukē emporion* of Ptolemy, the Pudu-chcheri or 'New Town' of the Tamils, garbled by Europeans as Puddicherry and Pondicherry. Shifting sands have moved the town a mile or two, but the name has come down, little changed, through nineteen centuries.

Of the buildings of this New Town something is now known, although brick-robbers have upturned much of the site. At the northern or seaward end, beside the river and at water-level, was a large, simple brick structure upwards of 150 feet long, pretty obviously a warehouse. Further south were courtyards walled with brick and timber, containing stoutly constructed brick tanks and cisterns, drains, wells and soak-pits, the last made in a characteristically Indian fashion of superimposed terracotta rings. South again, a formidable brick revetment, sloped or battered and surviving to a height of six feet, was traced by Mr Casal for a distance of eighty yards eastwards from its broken end on the river bank and was interpreted as the side of a tank or reservoir, but may rather have been a defensive revetment. And still further south scraps of walling have come to light in the much-disturbed ground. The overall impression is that of storage-accommodation towards the mouth of the former estuary, backed by industrial quarters where, it may be supposed, the 'Agaritic' muslins which the *Periplus* mentions as an export of the region were made and dyed, and where beads and other objects of semi-precious stones, which litter the area, were assembled or worked. The administrative centre, temples, and dwellings of the town have not yet been identified.

Most of the brick buildings explored were constructed after the red-glazed Arretine ware had ceased to arrive from Italy, where its manufacture in the forms and fabric now in question came to an end about A.D. 45. On the other hand the importation of wine-amphorae seems to have preceded that of the Arretine and certainly continued after the Arretine had ceased. The main development of the port may in fact be ascribed approximately to the middle of the first century A.D., although its international usage must have begun nearly half a century earlier, if the depth of the deposit (nine feet) containing amphora sherds under the warehouse be taken as an index.[1] Moreover, some of the Arretine ware dates probably from the first quarter of the first century A.D. For the subsequent duration of the town we have at present insufficient evidence. In the industrial area where the tanks or dye-vats are situated there were two or more phases of reconstruction, but there was a general continuity in the main units of the plan, and sherds of Mediterranean amphorae occurred in all strata. In other words, the function and contacts of the site remained unchanged. To interpret these factors in terms of time is guesswork; a minimum of a century might appear to have been required by the renewals, but there seems to be no compelling reason to allow more than two centuries, and a terminal date soon after A.D. 200 is suggested.

The quantity of Western pottery in the relatively small

1. This deposit was largely alluvial mud and probably accumulated fairly rapidly.

areas uncovered is impressive (pls. 19, A and B). At least fifty sherds of Arretine, including four potters' stamps (VIBIE, ITTA, CAMVRI, C.VIBI OF) are recorded, and others have been found, mostly in the northern (warehouse) sector where, it may be supposed, the shippers and merchants were congregated. Of amphora sherds something like 150 are known to have been unearthed over a wider area; and incidentally an internal incrustation on some of the sherds has been shown by analysis to contain resin, a traditional component of certain Greek wines though here (as elsewhere) perhaps applied deliberately by the potters to render the vessels impermeable. Other wares which may have been imported from the West include above all an extensive group of flat-bottomed dishes of a hard, metallic pottery, whitish in section but with a polished slip blackened internally by inverted firing and with concentric rings of rouletting on the upper surface of the base (fig. 19). Local imitations of

Fig. 19. Rouletted dish from Arikamedu. ¼

this ware are distinguished by softer fabric and coarser rouletting. This 'rouletted dish' is widely distributed in southern and central India and has become what geologists would call a 'type fossil' in the dating of associated Indian cultures. It will be considered again at a later stage.

Roman glass, including a 'pillared' bowl of first-century type (fig. 20, p. 188), reached the site in small quantities, and fragments of at least two characteristic Roman lamps of early date have been noted. On the other hand, coins of the period, whether Roman or Indian, are completely absent. This is in accordance with the postulate, already discussed, that the imported currency was not as a rule circulated in India in the normal processes of monetary exchange, the country being economically unprepared for it.

The discovery of Arikamedu is in more than one respect a landmark in the study of Indo-Roman relations. For the first time it gives a habitation and a name to one of the *emporia* with which the literature and the coinage had in a more general way familiarized us. The quantity of the Mediterranean material produced by comparatively trifling excavation is a suggestive index of the extent of the international trade which used the place. This fact, with the early date of some of the material and the suddenness with which it is superimposed upon a purely native and local culture, has substantiated the essentially Augustan organization of regulated monsoon traffic; whilst the remoteness of the site, on the further side of India, emphasizes the range of this new organization, the powerful purpose with which it was reaching out eastwards to the sources of pearls and silk. The imagination of the modern enquirer kindles as he lifts from the alluvium of the Bay of Bengal sherds bearing the names of craftsmen whose kilns lay on the outskirts of Arezzo. Fom the woods of Hertfordshire to the palm-groves of the Coromandel, these red-glazed cups and dishes symbolize the routine adventures of tradesmen whose story may be set only a little below that of King Alexander himself.

Other sites in central and southern India have produced occasional evidence of direct or indirect contact with Roman things, but cannot at present be classed with Arikamedu. Reference has been made to the rouletted dishes which were first identified and dated there, and to their distinctively Mediterranean character even when they may in fact be local copies. This type, wholly foreign to Indian ceramic tradition, nevertheless 'caught on' in India and has become an invaluable index of date on many sites where other time-evidence is lacking or inadequate. Far from the coast in northern Mysore, on the great central plateau, it has been found with, and has helped to date, an Andhra town of the first and second century A.D. at Brahmagiri in the Chitaldrug district; and forty-five miles away in the same district it has appeared at Chandravalli where, appropriately, *denarii* of Augustus and Tiberius have likewise been found. The Andhra towns of Maski and Kondapur, also on the Deccan plateau, have produced similar sherds; whilst nearer the east coast at yet another Andhra city, Amaravati, more rouletted pottery has been gathered on the surface, and the same site is said long ago to have yielded Roman coins not otherwise specified. Here, beside the famous *stūpa* which provided the sculptures long exhibited on the main staircase of the British Museum, is a town site which from more than one standpoint would amply repay excavation. And away to the north-east, some seven hundred miles from Arikamedu, near the sacred temple-city of Bhubaneswar, the excavators of an ancient walled town known as Sisupalgarh have found sherds of the same ware. These widespread occurrences represent altogether but a brief period of fieldwork, and there is no doubt that our new 'type fossil' of the first century A.D. will acquire an increasing importance as time goes by.

Apart from the rouletted ware, red-glazed pottery which may be of Mediterranean origin is reported to have been found at Nasik, 100 miles north-east of Bombay. Similar ware has been recovered recently (1954-5) from an ancient town-site at Nevasa in the district of Ahmadnagar, about the same distance east of Bombay, together with at least four Graeco-Roman amphorae which show a resinous coating on the interior.[1] A similar internal coating was observed on some of the Arikamedu sherds and may be ascribed to one of two causes: either it represents sediment from one of the resinous wines still familiar in Greece, or it is a deliberate application by the potter to ensure the non-permeability of the jars. Many of the amphorae recently brought up from the Greek wreck at Le Grand Congloué near Marseille were coated internally with a similar dark resinous or tarry substance which extended above the level of the cork in the neck of the jar and cannot there have been a product of the contents.

From another site not far from the Bombay coast comes a bronze statuette of Neptune or Poseidon and a Roman bronze jug of the middle of the 1st century A.D. (pls. 20 and 24A). They were found together in a brick building of Andhra date in an ancient town-mound at Kolhapur in the southern part of Bombay province, and are striking evidences of the trade which, as our historical authorities indicate, used a number of harbours on the Konkan coast, south of Bombay. When last seen by the writer in 1948 the jug and statuette were housed in a little museum at Kolhapur. The statuette is of better quality than the average commercial product and, perhaps with the Harpocrates

---

1. Information and drawing from Dr H. D. Sankalia.

from Taxila (p. 189), is the most noteworthy work of its kind from the East.

A little further north, at Akota in Baroda State, the bronze handle of a similar jug bearing a figure of Cupid (pl. 21A, c) has been discovered recently during the excavation, by the Baroda University, of the ancient site of Ankottaka. It is closely comparable with the handle of the jug from Hoby (pl. 7A) at the other end of the Roman map. From Karvan in the same state a cameo of exuberant sub-classical workmanship has also been recovered (pl. 21B), but details are at present lacking.

Also from central India, generally from the territory of the Andhra empire, come a number of imitations of Roman coins, made locally as ornaments and mostly pierced or looped for suspension. They are normally of terracotta and were doubtless originally gilded. The most remarkable series was unearthed at the Andhra town of Kondapur in Hyderabad State and is preserved in the Hyderabad (Deccan) museum (pls. 22 and 23). It consists of at least twenty recognizable imitations of *aurei* or *denarii* of Tiberius (d. A.D. 37), with an Indianized version of the head of the emperor on the obverse and of Livia as Pax on the reverse. Both sides bear garbled inscriptions. Two similar clay *bullae*, one of them again imitating a Tiberius (with Livia-Pax facing the wrong way, as befits a copy), were found at the Chandravalli site already mentioned. Another, also of clay, was dug up on the Kolhapur mound, and yet others bearing romanized heads come from Ujjain and Sisulpalgarh, and even from Rajghat on the outskirts of Benares, further north. A stone mould for casting a metal medallion of this class was found long ago at Besnagar, near Bhilsa in Gwalior State, and two gold medallions of sub-classical type and pierced for suspension were recovered at Nagarjunikonda in the Guntur district from a

Buddhist *stūpa* ascribed to the second-third centuries A.D. Another pierced gold imitation of an issue of Antoninus Pius was found with a pierced genuine *aureus* of Commodus at Chakerbedha, Bilaspur district, C.P. This list is not complete but sufficiently indicates the astonishing vogue of Roman coin-types over a large part of central India in the first and second centuries.

At the same time be it emphasized that, for all the vigour of its impact, the Roman trade implied by these odds and ends had no appreciable or durable effect upon the cultures of the peninsula. It left a superficial imprint here and there, sometimes in remarkably remote places, but nowhere south of the Vindhyas was that imprint more than a graffito upon an essentially self-sufficient native fabric. Only when we move northwards towards the foot-hills of the Himalaya do we find evidences of a more significant and lasting penetration of Western ideas, and to this difficult problem we must now turn.

CHAPTER THIRTEEN

PAKISTAN AND AFGHANISTAN

UNLIKE the south, India north of the Vindhya Range produced no great quantity of goods of the kind demanded by the Mediterranean market. Cotton was grown there, and the carnelian of Rajpipla was doubtless in some request then as now. But it is primarily as a channel for trade in transit from remoter sources that north-western India comes into the present story. The *Periplus*, as we have seen, includes turquoise, lapis lazuli, 'Seric' skins, and silk amongst the exports from the Indus delta, and these commodities have nothing in origin to do with the lands south of the Himalaya. Turquoise is above all a product of northern Iran; lapis lazuli comes from Badakshan, in the north-eastern corner of Afghanistan; the Seres, elsewhere associated with the silk and iron trade, are vaguely central or eastern Asiatic, and the skins described as Seric are evidently thought of as derived from High Asia; silk yarn was itself at this time a Chinese monopoly. For all these wares the direct passage to the West would have been the so-called Silk Route, across Iran to Syria. Astride this route, however, stood the implacable barrier of Parthia. Always in active rivalry and often at war with the Roman empire, Parthia blocked the Orient trade by extortionate levy or actual veto. The well-informed Chinese chronicles record that the Roman 'kings always desired to send embassies to China, but the An-hsi [Parthians] wished to carry on trade with them in Chinese silks and it is for this reason that they were cut off from communication'.[1] Thus save

1. F. Hirth, *China and the Roman Orient* (Leipzig, etc., 1885), p. 42; F. J. Teggart, *Rome and China* (Univ. of California, 1939), p. 145.

when on rare occasions a successful Roman campaign
momentarily reopened the western sector of the Silk Route,
this ceased to operate as a main artery of trade. It passed
indeed out of Western knowledge; so much so that after
Trajan's advance to the Tigris early in the second century
it was found necessary to explore the route afresh, if, as
seems likely, we should ascribe to this period the pioneer
mission sent by a Macedonian merchant, one 'Maës called
also Titianus' to the Stone Tower (Tashkurgan, between
Yarkand and Badakshan) and thence to 'Sēra, the metropolis of the Seres'.[1] With the journey of Julianus's knight
to the Baltic (p. 23), this enterprise ranks amongst the great
adventures of Roman commerce.

The Maës episode alone sufficiently emphasizes the normal insignificance of the main overland route through
western Asia in Imperial times. Whether or to what extent
a route further north from the Oxus by way of the Caspian
to the Black Sea was found more practicable we do not
know. The Asiatic connexions of the Greek cities of South
Russia suggest the possibility of easier access along it,
but evidence is at present lacking. Alexandria at least is
unlikely to have used it, and Alexandria was the focus of
the Orient trade. Nor, in the light of the *Periplus* and of
archaeology, is there room for doubt as to the main lines
of Alexandrian traffic with central Asia and China. They
lay through West Pakistan and northern India, where
geographical and political factors combined to facilitate
them.

First, geography. On the map, the Himalayan massif and
its extensions give the Indian sub-continent an aspect of
exclusiveness but are in fact penetrable at a number of
points. For example, there are routes from China to the
Brahmaputra in Assam, and it may have been along these

1. Ptolemy, I, II, citing Marinus.

routes that silk sometimes reached the coastal trade of the peninsula (p. 164). Through Sikkim it is possible to reach India from the Tibetan plateau. Further west a number of feasible if arduous routes enter Kashmir from Turkestan; the most notable of them used the famous Karakoram Pass, a desolate highway, if such it can be called, from High Asia into trans-Indus Kashmir. But neither this nor any other of these northern approaches has played any dominant rôle in the history of commerce. Their historical importance lay rather in another context altogether, as occasional channels for the diffusion of Buddhism from India to central Asia and China. The main entries lay on the north-western frontier of what is now Pakistan, and converge on the plain of Peshawar, using at first the line of the Kabul river and, from the second century A.D., the Khyber Pass.

Through these north-western gaps penetrated one of the great trade-routes of ancient Asia. It left the east-west trans-Asian Silk Route at Balkh, the little village which to-day represents Bactra, Mother of Cities, once a vast metropolis seven miles in circuit. Balkh lies on the steppe of Afghan Turkestan some twenty miles south of the Oxus, outside the former frontier of Parthia, and was a nodal point in the Asian traffic system. From it the old branch-route strikes south-eastwards to the Kabul river and India through clefts in the Hindu-Kush, thus circumventing the more formidable mountain-barriers further east. However devious, this is in fact the easiest highway from central Asia to north-western India. From China, says the *Periplus*, 'raw silk and silk yarn and silk cloth are brought on foot through Bactria to Barygaza.'

Secondly, the political factors. In the latter part of the first century the route just mentioned was adopted as the axis of advance by central Asian hordes under the leadership of one of their septs, the Kushans, who had overrun Bactria and now overflowed into India. The chronology of the Kushāna empire is still in dispute, but by the beginning of the second century A.D., if not earlier, it extended to the mouths of the Indus and far into the north Indian plains, thus unifying the political control of a vast tract of country from the Hindu-Kush to the sea and so, incidentally, simplifying and reducing Customs dues. Unlike their Parthian contemporaries, the Kushāna kings were singularly catholic in their political and cultural outlook and modelled their gold coinage (p. 169) – perhaps even some part of their religion – on that of the Roman West. There can be no doubt that the Western trade which passed through their territory was directly fostered by them. To that trade we must now return.

Be it repeated at the outset that, greatly simplified, the route followed by this east Asian trade was as follows (fig. 1, p. 14). From the Chinese province of Honan or thereabouts, tracks converged upon the upper valley of the Hwang Ho and thence proceeded by alternative courses, which do not concern us here, to Kashgar and Tashkurgan on the flank of the Pamirs, and so by the Oxus valley to Bactra. At Bactra the route divided in the fashion already indicated. Political conditions permitting, the traveller could continue westwards by way of Rhagae (Tehran) to Seleucia or Antioch. On the other hand, he could turn sharply south-eastwards to Pakistan and India, passing a number of trade-route cities of which Begram, forty-five miles north of Kabul and Taxila, on the borders of the Punjab and the North-West Frontier province of Pakistan, are for our present purpose the most important. From this sector the valleys of the Indus and its tributaries offered approaches to the Arabian Sea; or the journey could be continued, roughly along the line of the Grand Trunk Road, to the Kushāna capital of Mathura (Muttra), south of Delhi, and thence south-westwards through Ujjain to the port of Barygaza or Broach.

Many sites along this immense track-system must be capable of producing relevant evidence, but only two of them – those just mentioned – have been sufficiently explored to throw any considerable light upon the extent and character of the Western trade. Something must be said of each of them.

For more than twenty years Taxila has been submitted to large-scale excavation, and the results have been lavishly published.[1] Here it will suffice to observe that in the first century A.D. it was a walled city, now known as Sirkap, three-quarters of a mile in length, designed to include an acropolis on an intrusive, rocky headland, and a 'lower town' laid out in regular blocks or *insulae* on what may fairly be described as the Hellenistic pattern (pl. 25). It was at first under Parthian rulers who seem to have owed no allegiance to the central Parthian power in Iran; but soon after the middle of the century it passed to the Kushans and was, perhaps a century later, rebuilt by them a mile away to the north (now Sirsukh). Of the new foundation we have little knowledge, but it was the Sirkap city that straddled the period of the *Periplus*.

Comparison with the contemporary town of Arikamedu in the far south is at once inevitable and instructive. At Arikamedu, it may be recalled that a few months' excavation revealed a considerable mass of Mediterranean pottery – wine-jars, table-ware, lamps, even gems and glass. Many years of excavation at Taxila have yielded only a single wine-jar, three or four fragments of Western glass (fig. 20, 3), a gem or two, but not even a scrap of Arretine table-

1. J. Marshall, *Taxila* (Cambridge, 3 vols., 1951).

ware, not a single Roman lamp.[1] The contrast is significant.
There was at Taxila, unlike Arikamedu, no terminal trade
in the usual Mediterranean commodities, wine and crock-
ery. On the other hand, there were other contacts with the
West, of a kind which had in fact, as we shall see, a far more
enduring influence upon Asian thought or expression.

Fig. 20. Roman glass: 1, from Begram, Afganistan; 2, from
Arikamedu, S. India; 3, from Taxila (Sirkap), West Pakistan. ¼

1. From this generalization I exclude a few sherds showing
Hellenizing features in fabric or decoration which probably represent infiltration from western Asia, but have nothing to do with
the Italic imports of the main body of Augustan and post-Augustan
trade. The so-called 'Greek black ware' from Taxila is a widespread
North-Indian fabric, most if not all of which was doubtless made in
India itself.

Notable amongst these evidences is a charming bronze statuette of the child-god Harpocrates, his right forefinger raised to his lips possibly in a gesture of silence (pl. 1). On his head are the Egyptian crowns of the north and the south and, since the cult was centred upon Alexandria, the figure is likely to have come from there, in or about the first century A.D. A similar statuette will be noted from the Begram hoard (p. 194).

Other bronze and gold statuettes or reliefs from the site, such as a Cupid and a 'Venus', have been claimed as Graeco-Roman and owe something to Western influence but are probably of Indian manufacture. On the other hand, a silver repoussé *emblema* or circular decoration, representing Dionysus or Silenus, is a somewhat crude piece of Western workmanship (pl. 24B); it is probably from the centre of a dish, but, when lost, was mounted on a silver stand as a table ornament. With it was found a silver spoon with rat-tail ridge and cloven-hoof handle of Graeco-Roman type. Two or three bronze saucepans having tubular handles with ram's-head terminals are of similar derivation and are dated to the first century A.D. (again compare Begram, p. 194). Of the gems, two at least are imports from the Roman world: a gold-set carnelian bearing figures of Eros and Psyche with a small child, and a nicolo engraved with a winged cupid running after a bird and closely comparable with a gem from Arikamedu (p. 174). A *denarius* of Tiberius is also recorded, but otherwise Roman coinage is absent. A famous series of circular stone toilette trays show Western elements in their carved figure-groups, but are generally of Oriental workmanship.

These very various imports and derivatives tell a different story from the straightforward merchandise of the south. They hint at the casual acquisition of Western things; at opportunist purchase or levy from passing caravans carrying goods which may be broadly described as of the 'luxury' class. In view of the huge total extent of the material now available from Taxila, they do not suggest the purposeful and regular marketing of Mediterranean wares there. This conclusion will be discussed further at a later stage. Meanwhile, there is another aspect of the matter which must be touched upon in summary fashion.

An outstanding feature of the material recovered from Taxila and its environs is a considerable quantity of sculpture, in relief and in the round, in stone, clay, and, above all, stucco. If we set aside the innumerable small terracottas as secondary commercial products, the more monumental residue is still impressive in bulk, range, and sometimes quality. Most of it is derived from Buddhist shrines and monasteries; works of a definitely secular origin scarcely occur. More will be said at a later stage of the general problem which it raises. Meanwhile, examples of this art are cited to illustrate a specific character of some part of it – namely, a recurrent Western, Graeco-Roman element of a striking and significant kind.

The first is the stucco head of a smiling child (pl. 28B) from the monastery of Jaulian near Taxila. The head would be in place on any Graeco-Roman site, and has nothing in origin to do with the art of India. A similar comment is applicable to the stucco head of a fawn or satyr (pl. 28A), with pointed ears and snub nose, from the apsidal temple beside the main street of Sirkap (visible in pl. 25). Again the type is purely classical. A third example of the kind is the beautiful life-size stucco head of a youth from the Dhamarajika monastery at Taxila (pl. 29B). The head is unmistakably reminiscent of second-century Roman portraits, such as that of the youth Marcus Aurelius in the Capitoline Museum at Rome. Other Westernizing examples might be cited from Taxila, together with several in which the Western element is combined with Indian traits. Amongst the latter is a schist frieze from the Kunala monastery at Sirkap, showing *putti* and other figures amidst the serpentine loops of a continuous wreath with pendant grape-clusters pecked by birds. This classical motif – a recurrent one in north-western India at the period – shows, by the fleshiness of the figures and by some of the postures, the hand of the Indian carver, but is otherwise a non-Indian conception (pl. 26).

Outside Taxila, within the North-West Frontier Province of what is now West Pakistan and in adjacent Afghanistan, such Westernizing work is a familiar phenomenon. Thus from Charsada, on the Peshawar plain, comes a terracotta version of the Apollo Belvedere (pl. 29A), and from the same region is recorded a stone relief representing Laocoön, in Western costume, in the act of prodding the Trojan Horse, with a very Indian Cassandra in the background: a strange and revealing mixture of India and the Mediterranean with a distinctively Western theme (pl. 27). And again a stucco head of a warrior, also from the Peshawar district, recalls the typical Gaul of Roman art, whilst at the Buddhist site of Hadda in Afghanistan a reflection of the 'Antinous' type of second-century Rome is recognizable in the stucco figure of an effeminate youth, now at the Musée Guimet in Paris.

To these interchanges and resemblances between West and East we shall return. Before doing so, however, we must glance at another site, famous in consequence of its partial excavation by the French Archaeological Mission to Afghanistan between 1936 and 1942, under the direction successively of J. Hackin and R. Ghirshman.[1]

1. J. Hackin, *Recherches archéologiques à Bégram* (Mémoires de la Délégation Archéologique Française en Afghanistan, IX, 1939); R. Ghirshman, *Bégram, Recherches archéologiques et historiques sur les Kouchans* (Cairo, L'Institut Français d'Archéologie Orientale, 1946).

Some forty-five miles north of Kabul, at the junction of the rivers Ghorband and Panjshir beneath the towering range of the Hindu-Kush, are the remains of an ancient town now known as Begram, but formerly, as it seems, the Kapisi, royal capital of Kapisa, visited by the Chinese Buddhist pilgrim Hiuan-tsang in A.D. 644. It lies, as already mentioned, beside the branch-route from Bactra to India. The site itself falls topographically into three parts. Dominating the actual confluence is an area of about 150 × 100 yards known as the Bordj-i-'Abdullah or alternatively as 'the Ancient Royal Town', fortified by an earthen rampart revetted externally and internally with unbaked brick. Inadequate excavation has suggested that this may be the work of Graeco-Bactrian kings of the second century B.C. About 350 yards to the south, at the head of a gentler rise, is another oblong fortified area, 280 × 80 yards in extent, known as 'the New Royal Town'. The slope between the two enclosures also had lateral defences, but is unexplored.

Present interest centres upon the New Royal Town, where three main phases of occupation, ranging from the first or second century B.C. to the fifth A.D., have been identified. The first phase dates, perhaps, from the Indo-Greek kings, and to it belong stalwart fortifications of unbaked brick on stone footings, with rectangular salients or towers at frequent intervals and two ditches. On the southern side was a central gate which has not been planned. Within there is a hint, but no more, of a rectilinear lay-out as at Taxila (Sirkap). The phase was succeeded without visible break by Phase 2, ascribed to the great Kanishka in the second quarter of the second century. The new régime was marked by fresh buildings and repairs to old ones and, in particular, included a 'palace' of which more will be said presently. Ghirshman has made a good case for ending the second phase with the conquest of the territory by the Sasanid king Shapur I about A.D. 250, basing his conclusion upon evidences of violent destruction, coins, and a tomb-inscription at Naqsh-i-Rustam near Persepolis in Iran, which indicates that Shapur extended his empire to the Indus. After a brief interim, the city was partially rebuilt and, so far as excavated, appears to have been destroyed finally by the White Huns after A.D. 450. The whereabouts of the town visited by Hiuan-tsang two centuries later has not been ascertained.

Two rooms in the 'palace' of the second phase produced a hoard of Mediterranean and Oriental wares the like of which has not been seen elsewhere in Asia. At least one of the doors had been blocked up anciently, and there is no doubt that the objects had been carefully stored and were not in actual use at the time of the destruction. Thus in the north-western quarter of one of the rooms were placed glass vessels from Syria or Egypt, whilst in the centre and southern part were coffers and plaques of carved bone and ivory from India. Elsewhere was a group of bronze bowls from Western factories, and a cluster of steelyard-weights in the form of Minerva or Mars (pl. 30A). Elsewhere again were the remains of lacquer bowls from China. From the ends of the earth – from the West, from the Far East, from India – exotic things of beauty and worth had been gathered into the few square yards of these two sealed rooms, as so much bullion into a bank strong-room.

Associated Kushāna coins, including at least one of Kanishka himself and ending with the last king of the 'second Kushāna dynasty', Vasudeva, indicate the general period covered by the assemblage – namely, the second century A.D. and the earlier half of the third. The component parts, and in particular the Western glass which ranges in type from the (end of the) first (fig. 20, 1, p. 188) to the

G

third centuries, tally. In other words, the hoard is not an integral deposit, but an accumulation representing about 150 years. The easiest explanation is doubtless the correct one. The store was probably a Customs depot for the receipt of dues in kind collected by the kings or viceroys of Kapisa from the caravans which traversed the adjacent highway in the luxury traffic of Orient and Occident.

Let us for a moment glance at some of those wares which concern our special study. Statuettes of bronze include a little Harpocrates similar to that already described from Taxila and, like it, presumably from Alexandria;[1] a Hercules crowned with the Egyptian calathus and probably of similar origin (pl. 30B); a rider in classical garb (pl. 31B); and a grotesque 'philosopher' of the low-comedy type of which there are many examples in minor Roman art. The steelyard-weights in the form of classical busts have already been mentioned. Bronze feet from stands for lamps or incense or from caskets represent normal Western furniture; and bronze bowls identical with some of those which penetrated into Free Germany occurred here also in considerable quantity. Alabaster jugs and 'saucepans', the latter with ram's-head handle, are classical copies of normal metal forms. The glass includes a great number of familiar types, from the universal 'pillared' bowl of the first or early second century to a fine bowl of millefiori also of early date, a vase with a representation of ships and a lighthouse (tentatively identified by H. Seyrig with the pharos of Alexandria), painted and cut-glass goblets (pl. 31A), and vessels with semi-detached network surround. But most surprising in this remote spot is a number of plaster medallions, six to eight inches in diameter, bearing Mediterranean reliefs representing Minerva and other classical subjects,

1. P. 189. The Begram Harpocrates, now in the Kabul Museum, had had the right arm wrongly affixed when I saw it in 1946.

such as the vine harvest or Eros and Psyche, of a kind well known in the classical world (pl. 32). Such medallions were used as models by metal-workers, who transferred them to the silver dishes for which Alexandria and other Graeco-Roman centres were famous. Alexandria had special cause to use her vast local resources of plaster, and further reference will be made to the wider significance of this fact. If in regarding the Begram hoard we ignore the astonishing beauty of the great collection of carved ivory from India or the crumbling remains of lacquer work from China, and look only at these and other products of Roman Imperial crafts-manship, the spectacle, whether in the Kabul Museum or in the Musée Guimet in Paris, where a part of the collection can be seen, is one which stirs the imagination. And derelict Begram itself, where so little work has yet been done though with such dramatic result, remains a challenge to the explorer.

And now for certain wider issues. If one were asked to name the most penetrating and enduring impact of the Roman upon the Eastern world, the answer could scarcely be in doubt. In the early centuries of the present era the Buddhist art of north-western India and Afghanistan absorbed Western modes of expression, varying in kind and degree from instance to instance and from mind to critical mind, but constituting in the aggregate one of the most notorious and intriguing problems of art-history. Nor is the matter exclusively one of fashions and formulae. Eastern religious thought was itself undergoing at this time a process of change which presented significant analogies with the contemporary developments of Western metaphysics. The Western imperialistic idea and the Eurasian mysticism in which it was ultimately enveloped had appreciably close counterparts in the Orient; so much so that a good deal of nonsense has been written about the supposed interrelationship of Christianity and Buddhism, and may serve to warn us against an excessive affiliation of the respective arts. The main facts, however, are sufficiently clear. East and West were moving vaguely in the same direction, they had something of the same spiritual and aesthetic needs. Given the opportunity, there was every reason for a certain interchange or borrowing of material expression. And since 1870, when an official of the Punjab service brought to England from north-western India a small collection of 'Indo-Scythian' sculptures, it has been recognized that in and about the plain of Peshawar – the ancient Gandhara – and thence far afield in Asia a whole complex of Western ideas was in fact drawn at this time into the service of Buddhism.

Gandhara art, and that far wider art-province of which Gandhara provided a regional facet, does not concern us here in any detail. Its literature is immense and growing. The absence of an objective chronology has facilitated an infinite manipulation of the evidence in accordance with taste and theory, and until modern methods of excavation are applied to Buddhist sites far more rigidly than they have been in the past this source of doubt and disputation will remain.

Meanwhile, the governing principle may be emphasized that, with stray exceptions, this Romano-Indian art was confined to Buddhist patronage. Not only did the Buddhism of the age and place supply the religious and aesthetic context, but it also supplied the necessary wealth and backing. From the arrival of the Kushan dynasty in the latter half of the first century to the devastation of the whole region by the White Huns in the latter half of the fifth, Buddhism went from strength to strength, Buddhist monasteries multiplied across the landscape, and within the individual convents sculptured dedications jostled one another in ever-growing mass about the central shrine. For an understanding of this tumultuous manifestation a word or two must be said about the controlling faith.

Buddhism was in origin not a religion, but a philosophy of life. The Buddha, the Enlightened One, was not a god; he was an inspired teacher who, about 500 B.C., preached on the Ganges plains the Middle Path between indulgence and asceticism and sought an ultimate deliverance from accumulated sin in supreme detachment, *nirvana*. Later, however, by a process of evolution natural to a land where the teacher has always been revered, the Buddha was increasingly regarded as a divine Being to whom prayer might be offered. The earlier type of Buddhism is commonly distinguished as that of the *Hinayana* persuasion or the Buddhism of the Lesser Vehicle, and the later type (which did not wholly supersede the other) as that of the *Mahayana* persuasion or the Greater Vehicle. The latter persuasion reached maturity in and about the time of king Kanishka, who is now widely thought to have flourished in the second quarter of the second century A.D., about the time of Hadrian and Antoninus Pius in the West.

In artistic expression the outstanding difference between these two main types of Buddhism was that during the prevalence of the *Hinayana* teaching the Buddha himself was never represented. His presence was symbolized by a chair, a footprint, an umbrella, a riderless horse. About this symbol crowd the other participants in the scene, but there is no central commanding figure. In *Mahayana* Buddhism, on the other hand, the figure of the divine Buddha controls the assembly and is the focus of its composition. Both iconographically and aesthetically the change was revolutionary.

Artistically, this change found its first full expression in what is now West Pakistan and Afghanistan. The new Buddhism, amongst other faiths, received the patronage of the liberal-minded Kanishka, and the wealth of the Kushan empire provided a suitable environment for its development. What was lacking was any comprehensive traditional idiom in which to express the new observance; and it was here that Western art, already sufficiently familiar from the Western luxury trade described above – if not from the actual importation of Western craftsmen (p. 160) – came to the rescue. In the Roman Imperial West, the figure of the Roman emperor was established as the dominant feature of an artistic composition. Now, both this and some of its accessories and details, with others from Roman heroic and funerary art, were adapted to the Buddhist problem. Figures clad in Western clothing,[1] Western types such as *putti* or *erotes* and garlands, satyrs, Apollos, Minervas, even an occasional scene from Western legend such as that of the Trojan horse, and Western grouping such as that associated with the state arrival or departure of the Roman emperor, found their way into the sculptors' workshops of Gandhara and the adjacent region of Afghanistan. There they were to a greater or less extent transmuted by the Buddhist craftsman and given a Buddhist context. The fact that the region had previously been ruled by Indo-Greek kings may have, in some small degree, prepared the way for this influx. But it seems certain that, for more than two centuries before the Mahayana persuasion and its art took shape, the surviving Hellenism of Bactra had dwindled to vanishing point, and the most that it can have

1. The least Western of these figures is often the much-discussed figure of the Buddha himself. His monk's robe occasionally bears a more or less remote resemblance to the toga, but this resemblance is commonly exaggerated by modern writers, whilst the head is in most instances completely Oriental. It is in the details and grouping of subsidiary figures that Western iconography is more liable to intrude.

bequeathed to the subjects of Kanishka was a faint surviving sympathy for Western things. The idiom or 'language' of the new Buddhist art, in so far as it was non-native, was bred from new contacts. It was essentially a cultural by-product of the Kushāna commerce which brought into and through the kingdom objects and craftsmanship of the Roman empire.

As examples from Taxila have indicated, this Buddhist art has survived mainly in sculptural form, partly in stone, partly in stucco or plaster, and partly in clay. Most of the stone sculpture is carved in a green schist from the periphery of the ancient Gandhara. Its comparatively high 'survival value' and portability have tended to concentrate attention upon it and perhaps to exaggerate its relative importance. Far more widely spread in space, and probably in time, is the equivalent sculpture in painted stucco or clay, which is found not only in Gandhara, but far afield along the arterial routes that Buddhist monks shared with the traders through the Hindu-Kush and the Turkestans, along the China road. In Afghanistan the best-known source for this sculpture, mostly in stucco, but sometimes in stone, is Hadda, near Jalalabad, where there was a large Buddhist monastic settlement, but another monastery as far north as Kunduz on the Turkestan steppe in the same country has produced similar stuccoes, others are known in central Asia, and in the opposite direction stucco fragments have been found at Mohenjo-daro in Sind. It is observable that the stucco-medium, by reason of its easy manipulation, is associated with a greater range and vividness of expression than the stonework; and, on the other hand, that this facility, and the possibility of using moulds, encouraged mass production, particularly in the later and more decadent phases, when the use of the more laborious stone may have died out.

For the dating of this art there is little evidence. The earliest undisputed representations of the Buddha are those on certain gold coins of Kanishka, about or a little before A.D. 150, and this date accords well with what we know of the development of the Mahayana observance. A terminal date for the bulk of the surviving material in and about Gandhara is more securely fixed by the havoc wrought by the White Huns there during the half-century following A.D. 450. At Taxila a considerable quantity of stucco sculpture has been found in position in monasteries destroyed at that time and gives us a consistent picture of the condition of the art about the middle of the fifth century. We see that it was then highly stylized, but still retained traces of its dual (Eastern and Western) origin. The main brackets for this classicizing art in its homeland may be provisionally stated therefore as A.D. 100 and 450, though the tradition is still recognizable long after this period and in regions as remote as South India and the fringes of the Gobi Desert.

It remains to consider these various facts and probabilities in the general context of time and place. How did the Western elements reach the Gandhara studios? A part of the answer has been already given by Taxila and Begram. Behind the Western statuettes, glass, and stuccoes from those sites loom the presence and personality of Alexandria. Other Western workshops, notably those of Syria, doubtless contributed; but the dominance of Alexandria is scarcely in doubt. Long ago, before most of these discoveries were made, Rostovtzeff was able to affirm that 'the active agents in the exchange of goods between the Roman Empire and China were the Alexandrian merchants. Without them the commerce with India would probably not have existed.' More recently a growing knowledge of the art and craftsmanship of Palmyra has

pointed to a certain affinity of Palmyrene textiles and
jewellery with those of India, and occasionally to comparable traits, which may or may not be significant, between Palmyrene and Gandhara sculpture.[1] Such resemblances arise naturally from the known trade-connexions
of Palmyra with the Orient, but they merely supplement
the arterial traffic of Alexandria. Above all, Alexandria was
the principal home of stucco sculpture in the West.
Adjoining the city for miles the coastline is white with the
gypsum which is the raw material of stucco. And when in
Ptolemaic and Roman times (from the third century B.C.
forwards) statuary was demanded at Alexandria in con-
formity with Greek and Roman taste, the cheap local stucco
was extensively used as a substitute for the relatively costly
white marble which had to be imported from considerable
distances. There can be little doubt that it was the Alexandrian trade with and through the Kushan empire that
carried thither, not merely goods and ideas, but also the
stucco-technique; and that thereafter the use of this mobile
medium spread rapidly with the Buddhist monachism that
travelled northwards and eastwards with the caravans as
far as the border of China.

A rich and dominantly Alexandrian trade and a peculiarly receptive environment were, then, contributory
factors in the making of Romano-Buddhist art. It may be
doubted, however, whether they operated without a third
medium. Before A.D. 100 India was in intermittent diplomatic contact with the West – through the various missions
to which reference has been made (p. 161), and, by fair
assumption, through others unrecorded – and was actually

---

1. H. Seyrig, 'Ornamenta Palmyrena Antiquiora', in *Syria*, XXI
(1940), 305ff.; Rostovtzeff, *Revue des Arts Asiatiques*, VII (1931–32),
209; A. C. Soper, 'The Roman Style in Gandhara', in *American
Journ. of Archaeology*, LV (1951), 311.

employing Western craftsmen. The ancient story that King Gondophernes purchased St. Thomas as a slave in Jerusalem for the purpose of building his palace at Taxila may not be true, but must have been sufficiently possible to achieve acceptance; and more historical references to the reputation enjoyed by Yavana craftsmen employed in India are impressively numerous.[1] The suggestion that, on analogy, an occasional Western sculptor was similarly employed in Gandhara for training and assisting local craftsmen at a time of unprecedented demand is entirely consistent with this trend, and indeed completes the picture.

In summary, therefore, the basic explanation of Romano-Buddhist art in north-western India appears to be threefold. First, there were the new and congenial requirements of a *Mahayana* Buddhism backed by powerful patronage. Secondly, there was close commercial contact in high-grade wares, including sculpture in bronze and stucco, with the West and, in particular, with Alexandria. Thirdly, there is analogy for the direct employment of small numbers of Western craftsmen *in partibus*. To these factors may be added a fourth contributory factor in the incidental importation from Alexandria of a technique, that of stucco sculpture, which lent itself in a welcome measure to easy diffusion and mass-production. There the problem in its present limited setting may be left.

1. See above, p. 160, and A. C. Soper, as cited, p. 305.

CHAPTER FOURTEEN

THE FAR EAST

THE author of the *Periplus* was aware of lands beyond India, but knew almost nothing of them. East of the Ganges lay Chrysē, the Golden, 'the very last land towards the east.' Northwards was This, a land 'hard of access', with a great inland city called Thinae, whence silk was brought on the one hand to Bactria and Barygaza and on the other hand to the Ganges and South India. A century later, Ptolemy was able to collect extensive lists of place-names from the coasts, islands, and hinterland of these parts, but had little knowledge of their interrelationship. He was indeed misled by a basic conception that the Indian Ocean was a larger Mediterranean, south-eastern Asia being twisted southwards and westwards to join the coast of Africa somewhere south of Zanzibar. In the circumstances, it is not very profitable to spend time on an attempted reconciliation of his data with fact. His 'Golden Cherson-ese', like the Chrysē of the *Periplus*, may be equated with Burma and Malaya, and his 'Great Gulf' was probably the Gulf of Siam. In the Golden Chersonese he notes amongst other places two markets or *emporia*, Takola and Sabana, of which the former has been placed tentatively in the neighbourhood of Rangoon, where there is said to be some evidence of a place called Takkhala, Takola, or Tagala in the middle ages.[1] But only archaeological evidence can now give substance to identifications of this vague kind, and such evidence has scarcely been sought. That tangible evidence does in fact await discovery is suggested by the preliminary

1. On this point, and generally, see J. W. McCrindle, 'Ptolemy's Geography of India and Southern Asia', in *The Indian Antiquary* XIII (Bombay, 1884), 372, etc.; and McCrindle, *Ancient India as described by Ptolemy* (Calcutta, 1927).

excavation of an ancient town-site known as Oc-eo, fifteen miles from the shores of the Gulf of Siam, in Indo-China.

The site of Oc-eo lies by the delta of the Mekong river, on the fringe of the province of Long-xuyen, and is a complex of low mounds rising from the alluvial plain. The remains are those of a town framed by buried defences which form an oblong of rather more than 3,000 by 1,500 yards, with the considerable area of about two square miles. This area seems to have included timber huts (possibly on piles), and brick and stone buildings, together with rice-fields. Excavations were begun here in 1944 by M. L. Malleret on behalf of the École Française d' Extrême-Orient,[1] but have been curtailed by war conditions.

The excavator found remains of rectangular structures with flat roof-tiles, and more or less completely excavated two of them. One, of brick, consisted largely of closed cells which may (I suggest) have constituted the podium of a temple, comparable with the cellular podia characteristic of waterlogged sites of seventh century and earlier temples in Pakistan and northern India.[2] The other structure, of brick and granite, was identified as a *mandapa* or temple building with terracotta plaques bearing floral decoration and heads of monsters of a characteristically Indian type. Immediately flanking it were slight remains of two annexes, in one of which was part of a stone statuette of the Hindu god Vishnu. Other objects found during the excavations included relics of the cults of Siva, Vishnu, and Surya, traces of gold-, iron-, and copper-working, many thousands of beads of semi-precious stones, cameos of carnelian, crystal, or jasper bearing in some cases brief Brahmi inscriptions

1. Preliminary report in *Bulletin de l'École Française d'Extrême-Orient* XLV, fasc. 1 (Paris, 1951), 75ff, with other references.
2. R. E. M. Wheeler, *Five Thousand Years of Pakistan* (London, 1950), pp. 102-3.

of the second-fifth centuries A.D., fragments of bronze figurines, amongst which are noted Buddhist representations, a head and image in the Gandhara style and a statuette recalling the art of Amaravati, gold jewellery, and a wide range of terracotta ornaments. As a whole, the culture is half-native, half-Indian, and is appropriate to its peninsular location. But with these Indian elements are a number of objects or influences from further afield. Thus a blue glass gem bears in intaglio a bearded head with plaited hair and a Phrygian cap, probably of Sasanian origin. Other gems are regarded by the excavator as Roman: one bearing a cock on a chariot drawn by two mice, others with *grylli* or composite animals of a kind familiar in Roman art, others again with busts of Roman or romanizing type. A few of the beads are described as 'pseudo-Roman', but publication of them is awaited. No doubt at least attaches to a pierced gold coin of Antoninus Pius, dated to A.D. 152, and a second, less legible, of Marcus Aurelius.

All these Western elements should doubtless be ascribed to infiltration through India rather than to any more direct contact with the West. Nevertheless, it is a noteworthy coincidence that to the time of Marcus Aurelius the *Han Annals* attribute the arrival of an embassy from 'An-tun' (Marcus Aurelius Antoninus) at the Chinese court and the first opening up of intercourse with Ta-ts'in or the Roman Empire. The entry is as follows: 'They [the Romans] make coins of gold and silver. . . . They traffic by sea with An-hsi [Parthia] and T'ien-chu [India], the profit of which trade is tenfold. They are honest in their transactions, and there are no double prices . . . The budget is based on a well-filled treasury. . . . Their kings always desired to send embassies to China, but the An-hsi [Parthians] wished to carry on trade with them in Chinese silks, and it is for this reason that they were cut off from communication. This lasted till the ninth year of the Yen-hsi period during the Emperor Huan-ti's reign [= A.D. 166] when the king of Ta-ts'in, An-tun, sent an embassy which, from the frontier of Jih-nan [Annam], offered ivory, rhinoceros horns, and tortoiseshell. From that time dates the intercourse with this country.' [1] The *Annals* proceed to comment on the absence of jewels from the list of gifts offered by the 'embassy', and the comparative poverty of the tribute does in fact suggest the opportunism of some private merchant rather than a considered Imperial mission. Nevertheless, the episode, which is thoroughly circumstantial in its attendant details and is unlikely to have been invented, is a further example of the adventurous spirit in which Roman trade was conducted *in partibus*.

At the head of the Gulf of Siam, another site has hinted at indirect contact with the West. In the vicinity of P'ong Tuk, on the Mekong river forty miles from the coast, are the remains of Buddhist shrines dating apparently from the second-sixth centuries A.D. Indian influence is evident in the sculpture from the site, and may incidentally explain the presence there of a Roman bronze lamp of some distinction. The handle is a palmette between dolphins, and the lid bears in relief a head of Silenus crowned with ivy. [2] A date in the first or second century A.D. has been ascribed to the lamp, but may be too early. It is not impossible that the lamp reached the East during that ill-defined recrudescence of Romano-Oriental traffic which left an abundance of late fourth-century Roman copper coinage in southern India. [3] At any rate its presence in Siam may be

1. F. Hirth, *China and the Roman Orient* (Leipzig, Munich, Shanghai and Hongkong, 1885), p. 42.

2. G. Coedès in *Journal of the Siam Society*, XXI, pt. 3 (Bangkok, 1928), 204f. and pl. 19.

3. *Aspects of Archaeology* (*Essays to O. G. S. Crawford*), (London, 1951), p. 361.

ascribed to 'drift' rather than to organized intercourse with the West.

For the rest, Roman or sub-Roman wares, particularly glass, have been found from time to time in China. In south-eastern Korea two of the mounds which mark the burials of the kings of the local kingdom of Silla, broadly bracketed between 100 B.C. and A.D. 600, have produced glass vessels which may be Roman of the third or fourth century A.D. A glass dish, probably Roman, of about the same period is more vaguely recorded from Honan[1] and other early glass from China may include Western elements, though much more archaeological and spectrographic analysis is required before the extent of these elements can be estimated. If we accept the evidence of the *Pei-shih*, a relatively late version of earlier material, glass was not actually made in China until the second quarter of the 5th century A.D., when the process is said to have been introduced by traders from the country of Ta-yueh-chih, bordering on the north-west of India. Another version has it that the traders came from India itself. On the other hand it has been urged that certain Chinese glass beads resembling Western 'eye-beads', with the glass body inlaid with white rings and a coloured centre, indicate a partial introduction of the technique at a somewhat earlier date. Glass fragments found by Sir Aurel Stein in central Asia may indicate the line of approach, but once more the absence of precise detail is baffling. When China is once more accessible the whole problem is deserving of further attention. Meanwhile Rome in China remains the province of history – particularly of Chinese history – rather than of archaeology.

1. For these and other Western objects from China, the most accessible source is C. 'G. Seligman, The Roman Orient and the Far East', in *Antiquity*, XI (1937), 5ff.

CHAPTER FIFTEEN

RETROSPECT

ROMAN trade, diplomacy and 'drift' have now been traced, in however sketchy a fashion, far beyond the Imperial frontiers in Europe, Africa, and Asia. No attempt has been made to re-traverse in detail the ground covered in the recent past by Charlesworth, Warmington, or Eggers; on their basic work, and on their ancient authorities, the present book is founded. But here and there it has been possible to add to their material, to give it perhaps a new actuality and a new perspective. The French discoveries in Afghanistan and Indo-China, those of the British at Taxila and Arikamedu, or of the Italians in the Fezzan, have necessitated a partial rewriting of the story. On the old frontiers with Persia – in Syria, Iraq, Turkey, and Iran – a little new work has been done in recent years, but the evidence awaits full publication and synthetic treatment.

In conclusion, let us glance at the evidence as a whole and estimate very briefly the value of our material. Roman trafficking with lands outside the Empire was founded primarily on the supply of five commodities which were woven into the fabric of Imperial culture, and were essential in one way or another to the Imperial way of life. Free Germany produced the amber which was already an integral part of the equipment of southern Europe before the Empire was born. From tropical Africa came the ivory of infinite domestic use, either across the Sahara or by way of the Red Sea. Southern Arabia yielded the frankincense which had long been sought by the Pharaohs and the Achaemenids and, with gold and myrrh, was offered at Bethlehem. In peninsular India grows the abundant pepper which has for more than 2,000 years mitigated the cooking of the Western World. And China had a monopoly of silk until the sixth century A.D. Amber, ivory, incense, pepper, silk were the mainsprings of Roman long-range trade. The principal routes and markets were determined by them; a map of them is substantially a map of Imperial commerce as a whole. Into these routes and markets were fed, as was inevitable, a miscellany of other goods – pearls, semi-precious stones, tortoise-shell, muslin, skins, spices – which varied from place to place and served to enlarge business and make up cargoes. But all these things were supplementary to the Great Five, and an appreciation of this fact at once simplifies and rationalizes the complex story which otherwise is liable to baffle the reader.

Then, again, it may sometimes be worth while to distinguish, where possible, between deliberate, organized long-range trade and what may best be called 'commercial drift'. Trade in the five staple commodities was certainly organized. The *commercia* of the Baltic amber coast, the 'treaty ports' of the Orient, are illustrations, but the matter is not in doubt. How far, on the diplomatic level, the machinery of trade was an affair of the Imperial government, and how far it rested with the individual prestige and experience of the Roman shipping-companies is less certain. In the home waters of the Red Sea, direct government control was exercised; the centurion of Leukē Komē (p. 142) is good proof, and the licensed tax-collector Annius Plocamus exercised rights far round the Arabian coast (p.155). It may be that the 'Temple of Augustus' at Muziris (p. 147) indicates an official arm long enough to reach the Malabar Coast. But it may also be suspected that much of the more distant negotiation rested with commercial enterprise on a less formal basis, as in the earlier days of the East India Company. The so-called 'embassy' to the Chinese king in A.D. 166 (p. 205) has an unofficial ring about it, in spite of its pretension. And, as we have seen, the presence of sporadic Western goods at Oc-eo in Indo-China suggests mere drift in an intercourse essentially Indian rather than Roman in its structure. To drift likewise may be attributed the pots and coins which straggled on to the high plateau of the central Deccan and were sometimes copied there by local craftsmen. Most of the Roman goods from Free Germany were doubtless the product of drift from market to market or individual to individual, even when all allowance is made for diplomatic gift, such as is vouched for historically both in Europe and in Asia, or for military and tribal movement.

Each major discovery during the past twenty years has contributed, not only to the material content of our knowledge, but inferentially to the significant enlargement of our historical perspective in respect of these transfrontier contacts. In the Fezzan the Germa monument, for all its loneliness or even because of it, has about it the suggestion of something more than casual trading, and has here been recognized tentatively as a relic of a political agency disguised (as so often nowadays) in the shape of a technical mission (p. 131). Arikamedu or Podoukē, on the Bay of Bengal, has shown how, in the time of Augustus and Tiberius, Roman wine and table-wares were already reaching the far-off Coromandel coast in quantity, and the map of early Roman coinage across south India has pointed to the trans-peninsular route whereby they came from the harbours of Muziris or Nelcynda. The Arikamedu excavations have revealed for us how at this time a new commercial and industrial town sprang up here on the site of an insignificant village, and, with the help of the *Periplus* and Ptolemy, have illustrated the astonishing fashion in which, under the Principate, the shores of India – eastern no less than western – lit up with the beacons of a new international trade. And the Tamil literature has shown us vividly something of the foreign quarters of these harbour-towns, with their 'abodes of the prosperous Yavanas' and their 'sailors from many lands'. The Yavana sailors must mostly have been Egyptian Greeks and Arabs, but we may suppose that here and there a more or less resident freed-man represented the interests of a master sitting afar off in one of the shipping offices of Alexandria or Ostia, Myos Hormos or Berenice. To such accredited freedmen doubtless devolved the patient task of negotiating with local rajas and producers.

Two thousand miles further north, the excavations of Taxila and Begram have produced a different but no less revealing picture: of a rich trade in transit to and from further Asia, shedding samples *en route* in market or douane, but not chaffering to any great extent in these lands of passage. The two famous sites are complementary, and together constitute a formidable addition to the older evidence. Then, finally, the excavations of British, French, Japanese, and other archaeologists in Indo-China and central Asia have hinted at possibilities rather than produced finite information. There further evidence must be awaited.

From all this trafficking emerges a question of values which deserves some attention in the long view of history. To what extent were Western *ideas* diffused in the course of this vast diffusion of Western commodities? The importance of trans-frontier trade as a reflection of Roman enterprise and determination is manifest. Had it any more enduring consequence as a social or cultural stimulus in the lands to which it penetrated? More often than not the answer to this question must be 'No'. The Free Germans learned in one way or another to use Roman weapons and equally accustomed the Romans to the use of German or Scythian arms. The glamour of the Roman world, brought to their doors by trade and war, drew the migrating tribes and in some measure directed the refashioning of Europe; but it cannot be said that in its homes Free Germany was greatly influenced by contacts with Roman culture. The restless Garamantes of Africa may have been anchored temporarily in the interests of Rome by an imposed agricultural system and occasional trade, but their romanization, such as it was, had no long-term effect upon the cultures of inner Africa. The far more extensive contacts with South India have been a blessing to the archaeologist in search of fixed points for the dating of associated Indian cultures, but had no appreciable influence upon those cultures themselves. Only in the north, in north-western India (West Pakistan) and Afghanistan, have we found evidences of a fructual contact between West and East. There the combined accidents of the appropriate aesthetic and religious needs of the contemporary Buddhism, of a wealthy and powerful native regime favourable to that Buddhism, and of the diversion of much of the trans-Asian traffic of the West through the region by Parthian intransigence, brought the arts of the Mediterranean and of India together in a rare mutual understanding. Unless it be in the mingling of Muslim and Hindu traits in the medieval architecture of the same sub-continent, it is difficult to find another occasion on which so close an integration of two essentially alien traditions has been achieved. Disputation as to the precise manner of that integration – and disputation will continue until more exact evidence is forthcoming – cannot obscure the magnitude of the fact. And it is tempting to insist rather upon this positive instance of the transmission of ideas than upon the more negative transmission of pots and pence with which the bulk of our study, as of such studies generally, has been concerned.

Outside the immediate range of commercial and cultural values, a brave attempt has been made by an American historian[1] to fasten upon this international trade the responsibility for the major wars and migrations in Europe and Asia during the first centuries B.C. and A.D. and, by inference, over an indefinitely larger period. Within a selected time-bracket (58 B.C. to A.D. 107), the writer in question has tabulated, region by region from Britain to Cambodia, the known wars and disturbances, and has observed that every barbarian uprising in Europe followed the outbreak of war either on the eastern frontiers of the Roman Empire or in the 'Western Regions' of the Chinese. What is the significance of this coincidence? It is concluded that the correspondence of wars in the East and the invasions in the West was due to *interruptions of trade*, with Chinese aggression as a primary agency and Roman aggression as a secondary one. 'When war occurred on the routes in the Tarim basin, disturbances broke out in Parthia and either in Armenia or on the border of Syria. Evidently, then, war in the Tarim occasioned an interruption of traffic on the silk route, and this interruption aroused hostilities at points along the route as far west as the Euphrates. It seems highly probable, for example, that the invasions of Armenia by the Parthians, while Armenia was controlled by Rome, were inspired by the suspicion that the Romans had succeeded in diverting the movement of commodities from Central Asia to some route which avoided Parthian territory. But these secondary or derivative wars . . . brought about new interruptions of trade, and thus led to new wars in more and more distant areas. So interruptions of traffic on the Black Sea stirred up peoples north of the [lower] Danube, and the long train of disturbances ended finally in collisions of the barbarians with the Roman legions on

1. F. J. Teggart, *Rome and China* (Univ. of California, 1939).

the Rhine. Consequently, it is to be seen that people in no way concerned with the Silk Route might yet be connected with the interruptions of trade on that route through the hostilities which the interruptions precipitated between Parthia and Rome. . . .' In this theory the Silk Route and its extensions become an instrument of High Tragedy, of a forthright kind which by its very simplicity is suspect as an explanation of the complex workings of history. Other simple solutions of folk-disturbance have been sought from time to time in factors such as climatic fluctuation, evolving economy, overcrowding, personal or national ambition. These are facets of the problem, variously emphatic in varying circumstance; they are not its core, which is likely enough to lie embedded beyond the superficial view of history. Amongst them, trade-routes and commodities may be sufficiently stressed without the implication that history must be regarded persistently through a shop window.

SELECT BIBLIOGRAPHY

GENERAL

M. P. Charlesworth, *Trade-routes and Commerce of the Roman Empire* (Cambridge, 1926).

EUROPE

O. Brogan, 'Trade between the Roman Empire and the Free Germans', in *the Journal of Roman Studies* XXVI (London, 1936), 195ff.

H. C. Broholm, *Danmark og Romerriget* (Copenhagen, 1952).

H. J. Eggers, *Der römische Import im freien Germanien* (*Atlas der Urgeschichte* I, Hamburg, 1951).

H. Shetelig and H. Falk, *Scandinavian Archaeology* (Oxford, 1937).

AFRICA

G. Caputo and others in *Monumenti Antichi* XLI (Rome, 1951).

M. Reygasse, *Monuments funéraires préislamique de l'Afrique du nord* (Paris, 1950).

ASIA

M. P. Charlesworth, 'Roman Trade with India: a Re-survey', in *Studies in Roman Economic and Social History in Honour of Allan Chester Johnson*, ed. by P. R. Coleman-Norton (Princeton University Press, 1951).

W. W. Tarn, *The Greeks in Bactria and India* (Cambridge, 1951).

E. H. Warmington, *The Commerce between the Roman Empire and India* (Cambridge, 1928).

R. E. M. Wheeler, 'Roman Contact with India, Pakistan, and Afghanistan', in *Aspects of Archaeology, Essays presented to O. G. S. Crawford*, ed. by W. F. Grimes (London, 1951).

INDEX